Impact English

MIKE GOULD (SERIES EDITOR), KIM RICHARDSON, MARY GREEN & JOHN MANNION

Key Stage 3 – Year 8 • Student Book 2

Contents

Unit 1 Gothic horror

1 **Dracula** by Bram Stoker — 4
   Narrative — W5, S7, R14
2 **Alternative Endings to an Unwritten Ballad** by Paul Dehn — 12
   Poem — W11, R14
3 **Mad Vlad and Dangerous to Know** — 19
   Discursive — R10, S&L10
4 **Assignment: Gothic storyteller** — 25
   Narrative — AF3

Unit 2 Tales retold

1 **The Pig Scrolls** by Paul Shipton — 28
   Narrative — Wr6, Wr8
2 **How Urban Legends Work** — 35
   Explanation — S6, Wr11
3 **Living Legends: Robin Hood** — 42
   Analysis — S3, S&L2
4 **Assignment: The detective** — 49
   Analysis — AF3

Unit 3 Magic and illusion

1 **The Lord of the Rings** by J.R.R. Tolkien — 52
   Narrative — W11, R7
2 **The Nose** by Iain Crichton-Smith — 59
   Poem — R10, Wr7
3 **Derren Brown plays tricks** — 66
   Explanation — R3, Wr11
4 **Assignment: The magician** — 72
   Explanation — AF5

Unit 4 Destructive nature

1 **Tornado Alley** — 74
   Information — S4, R2, Wr10
2 **Tea Pests** by J.W. Beagle-Atkins — 81
   Recount — W11, S6, R3
3 **The Birds** by Daphne du Maurier — 88
   Narrative — S3, S10, S&L11
4 **Assignment: The weather forecaster** — 95
   Information — AF2

Unit 5 Family drama

1 Billy Elliot by Lee Hall		98
Film script	W7b, S&L14, S&L16	
2 Writing for The Simpsons		105
Recount	S6, R5, R8	
3 My Family: Review		112
Review	R6, Wr18	
4 Assignment: Drama reviewer		119
Review	AF2	

Unit 6 Refugees

1 Refugee Boy by Benjamin Zephaniah		122
Narrative	W1, R5, Wr17, S&L12	
2 Refugees and Asylum Seekers – the Facts		129
Information	W10, W14, R8, Wr17, S&L3, S&L10, S&L12	
3 STAR Campaign Leaflet		135
Advice	S7, S9, Wr15, S&L12	
4 Assignment: How to write to an MP		143
Advice	AF2	

Unit 7 New media

1 The Birth of The Bug		146
Persuasion	S9, R9, S&L4	
2 Don't Believe the Hype: The Internet's a Waste of Time		154
Argument	W14, R7, Wr14	
3 How to Make a Mobile For-tune		162
Recount	S1	
4 Assignment: The Internet is cool		169
Argument	AF3	

Unit 8 Voices from the past

1 Private Peaceful by Michael Morpurgo		172
Narrative	W11, Wr5	
2 The True Mystery of the Mary Celeste		180
Discursive	S4, S5, Wr16	
3 Roman Wall Blues by W.H. Auden		188
Poem	Wr17, S&L3	
4 Assignment: The soldier poet		195
Poem	AF1	

Unit 9 Dangerous pursuits

1 Extreme Sport		198
Information	S10, S12	
2 The Science of Bungee-jumping		205
Explanation	S8, R4, S&L4, S&L5	
3 Touching the Void by Joe Simpson		214
Recount	S1, S2	
4 Assignment: Explorer		221
Recount	AF3	

Unit 1 Gothic horror

 Dracula

- Read an extract from *Dracula*
- Learn what a Gothic story is
- Learn about Gothic language and sound effects (R14)
- Learn about different connectives of time and conjunctions (S7)
- Write in the Gothic style

The following extract is from Bram Stoker's *Dracula*. Jonathan Harker, Quincey Morris and friends are chasing Count Dracula, who will rise from his coffin when the sun sets. Quincey has been wounded. Jonathan's wife, Mina, is surrounded by a ring of fire – a holy circle – to keep her safe from Dracula. She narrates what happens next.

The waxen image

In the midst of this I could see that Jonathan on one side of the ring of men, and Quincey on the other, were forcing a way to the cart. It was evident that they were bent on finishing their task before the sun should set. Nothing seemed to stop or even to hinder them. Neither
5 the levelled weapons nor the flashing knives of the gypsies in front, nor the howling of the wolves behind, appeared to even attract their attention. Jonathan's impetuosity, and the manifest singleness of his purpose, seemed to overawe those in front of him. Instinctively they cowered aside and let him pass. In an instant he had jumped upon the
10 cart, and with a strength which seemed incredible, raised the great box, and flung it over the wheel to the ground. In the meantime, Mr Morris had had to use force to pass through his side of the ring of Szgany…As Jonathan, with desperate energy, attacked one end of the

chest, attempting to prize off the lid with his great Kukri knife, he attacked the other frantically with his bowie. Under the efforts of both men the lid began to yield. The nails drew with a screeching sound, and the top of the box was thrown back.

I saw the Count lying within the box upon the earth, some of which the rude falling from the cart had scattered over him. He was deathly pale, just like a waxen image, and the red eyes glared with the horrible vindictive look which I knew too well.

As I looked, the eyes saw the sinking sun, and the look of hate in them turned to triumph.

But, on the instant, came the sweep and flash of Jonathan's great knife. I shrieked as I saw it shear through the throat; whilst at the same moment Mr Morris's bowie knife plunged into the heart.

It was like a miracle; but before our very eyes, and almost in the drawing of a breath, the whole body crumbled into dust and passed from our sight.

I shall be glad as long as I live that even in that moment of final dissolution, there was in the face a look of peace, such as I never could have imagined might have rested there.

The Castle of Dracula now stood out against the red sky, and every stone of its broken battlements was articulated against the light of the setting sun.

The gypsies, taking us as in some way the cause of the extraordinary disappearance of the dead man, turned, without a word, and rode away as if for their lives. Those who were unmounted jumped upon the leiter-wagon and shouted to the horsemen not to desert them. The wolves, which had withdrawn to a safe distance, followed in their wake, leaving us alone.

Mr Morris, who had sunk to the ground, leaned on his elbow, holding his hand pressed to his side; the blood still gushed through his fingers. I flew to him, for the Holy circle did not now keep me back; so did the two doctors. Jonathan knelt behind him and the wounded man laid back his head on his shoulder. With a sigh he took, with a feeble effort, my hand in that of his own which was unstained. He must have seen the anguish of my heart in my face, for he smiled at me and said:-

'I am only too happy to have been of service! Oh, God!' he cried suddenly, struggling up to a sitting posture and pointing to me, 'It was worth this to die! Look! Look!'

The sun was now right down upon the mountain top, and the red gleams fell upon my face, so that it was bathed in rosy light.

waxen image small model person made of white wax
levelled aimed, directed
impetuosity rashness, hastiness
manifest clear, obvious
instinctively without a thought, naturally
bowie stout hunting knife
rude rough
vindictive desire for revenge
dissolution falling apart, death
battlements parapet at the top of a castle, with squared openings for shooting
articulated in the text it means that all the structure is displayed
leiter-wagon leading wagon
feeble weak

Key Reading

Narrative texts

This text is an extract from a **narrative**. Its **purpose** is to tell a story.

The main features of this text are:

- It has a structure that includes an opening (**introduction**), a problem (**complication**), a dramatic moment when everything comes to a head (**crisis**) and an ending (**resolution**) when things are sorted out. For example, *Dracula* has the following structure:

  Introduction: Jonathan Harker, a lawyer, is asked to visit a mysterious Count Dracula who lives in Transylvania.

  Complication: While there, Jonathan discovers that the Count is a vampire. Dracula sets sail for England determined to seduce Jonathan's wife-to-be (Mina) and friend (Lucy).

  Crisis: Lucy becomes a vampire. Jonathan and his friends must release Lucy's soul, save Mina from Dracula and rid the world of him.

  Resolution: Dracula's throat is cut and a knife is plunged into his heart.

- It has **characters**, who the story is about. The reader often hears their words and thoughts.

- It has a **narrator**, who tells the story in either the first person (I/we) or the third person (he/she/it), for example, Mina is the narrator of the extract: '*I saw the Count lying within the box…*' is a first person narrative.

- It uses **powerful words**, so that the language of the narrative is interesting to read or listen to, for example, 'The Castle of Dracula now stood out against the *red sky…*'

1 What is the most important thing that happens in the extract?

2 Name three of the characters.

3 a) Is the text told mainly in the first person or the third person? Give reasons for your answer.

b) The extract sometimes shifts to the other person. Find an example of this.

4 Find another example of powerful description in paragraph 1.

Purpose

The purpose of a narrative is to entertain us. One way to do this is to keep the reader's attention. For example, in paragraph 2 the description of Dracula makes the reader want to find out what he might do.

5 Read paragraphs 3 and 4 (but not paragraph 5). What do you want to find out here? Make a list.

6 Decide on the two most important things you want to find out as you read the rest of the extract. Consider:
- what happens to Dracula
- what happens to the other characters.

Reading for meaning

The Gothic style

A Gothic tale is a tale of horror.

- **Settings** for Gothic tales are dramatic and from the past. For example, ruined castles, secret places and sweeping landscapes.
- **Characters** express strong feelings and desires. They may have nightmares, see visions or go mad.
- **Events** in the plot are also dramatic: there may be a kidnapping or an imprisonment under the power of some evil presence.
- The **language** used in Gothic writing is usually **sensational** (causing feelings of surprise or horror). This creates an air of fear and mystery, and suits the dramatic plot.

The following example from *Dracula* is written using sensational language. Quincey Morris has been badly wounded and Mina is by his side.

> 'I am only too happy to have been of service! Oh, God!' he cried suddenly, struggling up to a sitting posture and pointing to me, 'It was worth this to die! Look! Look!'

Now read the example again, which has been rewritten in a non-Gothic style:

> 'I am only too happy to have been of some use,' he whispered. Then attempting to sit up he pointed towards the sunset. 'Look,' he said, 'it was worth it.'

7 Find as many differences as you can between the two examples above. Look at:
- words that have been replaced in the non-Gothic example
- words that have been left out or turned around
- the punctuation.

Exploring further: Alliteration

Alliteration, which is usually found in poetry, is sometimes used to make the Gothic style more sensational. It can create creepy sound effects: for example, when the same letter is repeated at the beginning of words, as in '*s*ilent *s*leepers'.

8 Find three examples of alliteration in the text.

9 Read examples A and B below. Which is written in the Gothic style? Work in groups and find four pieces of evidence to support your decision.

A
> My pulse was beating, my heart racing! But the creature – seeming to bear down upon me with its great paws – instead rushed headlong towards the chasm. That perilous pit! There, in one mighty leap, the beast spanned the abyss and in an instant, had vanished! Vanished into the forest!

B
> My pulse and heart were racing, as the creature gaining speed had almost caught up with me. But instead of sweeping me up in its great paws it flew past, making for the chasm. In one mighty bound the creature had leapt across and almost as quickly had vanished into the forest.

Focus on: Linking by time

Using **paragraphs** is an important way to link ideas in a text. In a Gothic narrative, paragraphs are sometimes linked by **connectives** that show several things happening at the same time. This increases the drama of the narrative. For example, paragraph 2 starts with a description of Count Dracula in his coffin. Then paragraph 3 begins:

Refers to events happening at the same time as those in paragraph 2

S7 **10** Find an example of this use of connectives in paragraphs 4 and 7.

11 Different time connectives link paragraphs by showing *what happens next*. Which time connectives start these two paragraphs?

A
> After the horses were ready Rudolpho helped her into the waiting carriage. He cracked the whip and they began their long and dangerous journey. While they kept to the main track…

B
> A moment later she heard a sound she had never heard before. It was like…

Exploring further: Conjunctions

Sentences written in the Gothic style are often long. Sometimes **conjunctions** are used to lengthen sentences. Conjunctions are a type of connective that can link different clauses in a sentence. For example:

> The sun was now right down upon the mountain top, **and** the red gleams fell upon my face…

'and' is the conjunction that links two clauses to make one compound sentence

12 a) Which conjunctions in the following sentences link the two clauses?

- There was a cloud of dust and the coffin disappeared.
- The scene was terrifying yet I had to turn back.

b) Add another clause to both of the above sentences using the following linking conjunctions: 'although', 'because', 'after'.

Key Writing

13 You are a writer of Gothic tales. Your task is to:

a) Continue the two paragraphs from question 11. You should consider these questions:
- What happens next on the journey?
- What does she hear?

b) Add a third paragraph to end the journey dramatically. Start this paragraph with a **time connective** that shows what happens next.

Remember:

- Include **sensational language** to give the tale some Gothic style. For example, you could include baying wolves, towering snow-capped mountains, or a strange and murky light.
- Use **conjunctions** to extend your sentences in Gothic fashion. For example, 'but', 'before', 'since', 'until', 'while', 'when'.

2 Mrs Ravoon

Aims

- Read the poem, *Alternative Endings to an Unwritten Ballad*
- Learn about Gothic writing and archaic words (R14)
- Learn about comic poetry, word associations and rhyme (W11)
- Build a character and a setting
- Write a poem

Many vivid images spring to mind when reading this poem by Paul Dehn. As you read it you will realise that each verse has a different setting and is like a different ending for a Gothic poem.

Alternative Endings to an Unwritten Ballad

I stole through the dungeons, while everyone slept,
  Till I came to the cage where the Monster was kept.
There, locked in the arms of a Giant Baboon,
  Rigid and smiling, lay…MRS RAVOON!

5 I climbed the clock tower in the first morning sun
  And 'twas midday at least 'ere my journey was done;
But the clock never sounded the last stroke of noon,
  For there, from the clapper, swung MRS RAVOON!

I hauled in the line, and I took my first look
10 At the half-eaten horror that hung from the hook.
I had dragged from the depths of the limpid lagoon
  The luminous body of MRS RAVOON.

I fled in the storm, the lightning and thunder,
   And there, as a flash split the darkness asunder,
Chewing a rat's-tail and mumbling a rune,
   Mad in the moat squatted MRS RAVOON!

I stood by the waters so green and so thick,
   And I stirred at the scum with my old, withered stick;
When there rose through the ooze, like a monstrous balloon,
   The bloated cadaver of MRS RAVOON.

Facing the fens, I looked back from the shore
   Where all had been empty a moment before;
And there by the light of the Lincolnshire moon,
   Immense on the marshes, stood…MRS RAVOON!

---

ballad a story in verse
clapper the striker or tongue of a bell
limpid clear
luminous bright and shining
asunder (old-fashioned term) apart
rune a mark or letter of magic or mysterious importance
cadaver a corpse
fens marshland

Key Reading

> **Poetry**
>
> This text is a **poem**. Its **purpose** is to explore feelings and ideas. A poem is made up of **images, rhythm** and **form**.
> - The **images** are the pictures made by the words.
> - The **rhythm** is like the beat in music.
> - The **form** is the framework or pattern of the poem. Poems are written in **lines** not sentences.
>
> Other important features of poetry are:
> - Some poems **rhyme**. For example, in *Alternative Endings to an Unwritten Ballad* the words 'slept' and 'kept' rhyme.
> - Some poems are **free verse**. They have lines of different lengths with different rhythms. (Some free verse contains rhyme.)

1. Who or what is the poem *Alternative Endings to an Unwritten Ballad* about?

2. What kinds of setting are mentioned in the poem?

3. The rhythm of the poem is the same in each verse. In other words, it has a regular rhythm. Find three other things that are regular or repeated.

4. Find two dramatic images of Mrs Ravoon.

Purpose

5. **a)** What is the main reason why this poem was written? Choose from the following options and give a reason for your choice:
   - to frighten the reader
   - to make the reader laugh
   - to make fun of the Gothic style
   - to explore what ghosts are
   - to explain what happened to Mrs Ravoon.

   b) Which of the other purposes are also true of the poem?

Reading for meaning

Gothic tales of horror and the supernatural often take place in the distant past. They are also written in a very dramatic style, so they are easy to make fun of, as the poet does in this poem. For example, when you hear the name 'Dracula' you probably think of 'vampire'. This is because the word 'Dracula' carries particular **associations** for the reader. However, when you hear the name 'Mrs Ravoon', a picture of a ghost probably does not spring to mind.

6 What picture does the name 'Mrs Ravoon' conjure up in your mind? Discuss your ideas with a partner.

In the poem, the reader never knows who or what Mrs Ravoon really is or where she comes from. However, there are clues that help to build up a picture for the reader.

7 Identify the word in the glossary that gives specific information about Mrs Ravoon.

8 a) Read the first verse of the poem again. Find key words that give the reader more information about Mrs Ravoon.

b) How does the word 'rigid' fit with your answer to question 7?

9 a) Use the key words you have identified in the first verse to build up a picture of Mrs Ravoon. Use a spidergram like the one below.

b) Check the last two lines of the other verses for more words that describe Mrs Ravoon. Add them to your spidergram.

10 Write three sentences describing Mrs Ravoon, using the information from your spidergram.

Exploring further: The Gothic setting

Gothic tales are often set in wild and dangerous places. However, the setting in the poem *Alternative Endings to an Unwritten Ballad* changes in each verse.

11 Draw another spidergram that shows each of the settings. For example,

Focus on: Rhyming associations

Athough the name 'Mrs Ravoon' is funny, it also has associations with 'death' through other rhyming words. For example, 'Ravoon'/ 'tomb'/'doom'.

12 a) Add any words that rhyme, or almost rhyme, to make a longer chain. You may like to use a rhyming dictionary.

  b) Now do the same with the following words:

  - mean
  - spell
  - sore
  - flinch
  - blood.

Keep your rhyming words ready for question 14.

Exploring further: Archaic language

The poem *Alternative Endings to an Unwritten Ballad* includes **archaic language**. This means words or phrases that are out of date – they were once used in English but are no longer used. For example, 'ere' is an old word meaning 'before'.

13 a) Find another example of archaic language from the poem and write down its meaning.

b) What do you think the following words mean?

- oft
- thou
- yonder
- cometh

Write down your answers.

c) Why do you think that archaic language is included in the poem? (Look at 'Reading for meaning' on page 15 for clues.)

Key Writing

 14 Refer back to the spidergram you created for Mrs Ravoon in question 9. Working in groups, make another spidergram – this time for a vampire.

a) Brainstorm a name for your vampire. The name should have associations with death or the supernatural. For example:

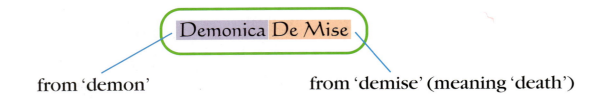

from 'demon'   from 'demise' (meaning 'death')

Write the name of your vampire at the centre of your spidergram.

b) Brainstorm ideas about what your character is like. Add these around your vampire's name on the spidergram.

c) To gather useful vocabulary, look up key words in a thesaurus. Start with Gothic words from the poem and then use the following words:

- fang
- coffin
- blood
- graveyard
- sunset
- fright.

Add any words that suit your vampire's character to the spidergram.

15 Working on your own, choose to write **either** Option A or Option B below.

Option A:

Write the last verse of a poem in which you see the vampire. Follow the verse pattern of *Alternative Endings to an Unwritten Ballad*. You could begin:

'Far below in the pit, where the sun never reaches…'

Remember:

- Don't force the rhymes. Choose those that fit the meaning best. Look back at the rhymes you made for question 12, to see if there are any you can use.
- Break the rhyme pattern if you wish; for example, at the end of the last line.
- Keep the rhythm of the lines regular.

Option B:

Write a description and include your vampire character in a Gothic setting. Look back at your work on Gothic settings from question 11. You could begin:

- 'I was surrounded on all sides by…'
- 'Suddenly I looked up and saw, towering above me, a creature with…'

3 Vlad the Impaler

- Read a discursive text about Vlad the Impaler
- Identify points 'for' and 'against' an issue
- Identify evidence in the text
- Discuss and present a point of view (S&L10)

Who exactly was Vlad the Impaler and why is he often associated with Dracula? Read the following and find out.

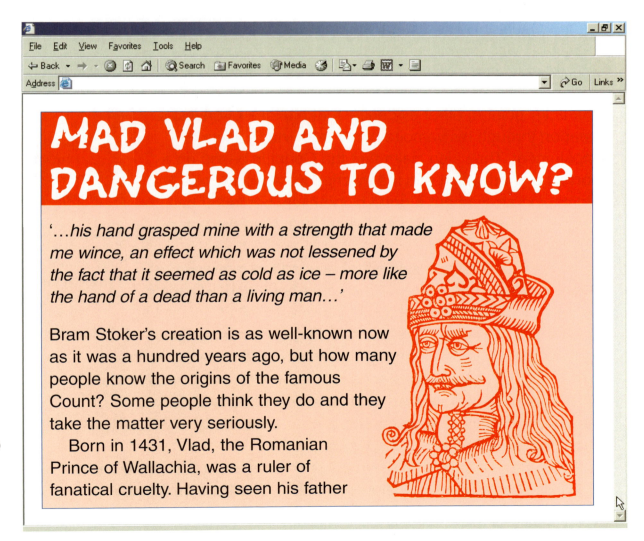

MAD VLAD AND DANGEROUS TO KNOW?

'...his hand grasped mine with a strength that made me wince, an effect which was not lessened by the fact that it seemed as cold as ice – more like the hand of a dead than a living man...'

Bram Stoker's creation is as well-known now as it was a hundred years ago, but how many people know the origins of the famous Count? Some people think they do and they take the matter very seriously.
   Born in 1431, Vlad, the Romanian Prince of Wallachia, was a ruler of fanatical cruelty. Having seen his father

murdered, his brother tortured and been imprisoned himself, he wreaked havoc on anyone who crossed his path. Many of his victims were subjected to a painful death. They were flayed alive, boiled in oil, beheaded, burnt, chopped into pieces or had wooden stakes driven through their bodies. His castle was surrounded by impaled corpses. Impalement seems to have been his preferred method of torture and he became known as Vlad the Impaler.

But how far did Bram Stoker base his vampire on Vlad? There is certainly evidence to suggest that he knew of his existence. In 1890, while on holiday in Whitby, Yorkshire, where much of the novel is set, he discovered William Wilkinson's book *An Account of the Principalities of Wallachia and Moldavia* and a reference to a warrior Dracula. It was from this he chose the name for his novel. Interestingly Vlad went by (or was given) the name 'Dracul'.

Those who are convinced that Vlad is Bram Stoker's character point to other evidence: that his idea of driving a weapon through his vampire came from Vlad's liking for impalement. They also claim that the Count is based on a portrait of Vlad which has the inscription, 'A wonderous and frightening story about a great bloodthirsty berserker called Dracula'. Some have even suggested that Vlad drank his victim's blood.

However, it is also possible that beyond the reference to Dracula, Bram Stoker knew little more about Vlad. Elizabeth Miller* points out that nowhere in the novel is Vlad referred to, nor are any of his habits recounted. To draw a connection between driving a stake through a vampire and impaling victims is too far-fetched, she suggests. As for the portrait, what proof is there? Bram Stoker may have read countless descriptions of Gothic characters. Finally, she claims there is no evidence in any historical data that refers to Vlad as a vampire.

So, is Vlad Dracula and Dracula Vlad? Or is Bram Stoker's creation the work of a fertile imagination with a little help from the Whitby public library? You can decide.

* See Introduction to: *Lord of the Vampires* by Jeanne Kalogridis (1997)

---

wince to shrink or give a start back
fanatical excessive
wreak to cause or inflict
havoc chaos, destruction
flay to strip off the skin
impale to pierce with a pointed stick
principality the territory or land belonging to a prince
inscription words carved or engraved on something
beserker violent warrior

Key Reading

> **Discursive texts**
>
> This text is a **discursive** text. The **purpose** of discursive writing is to present an argument from different points of view.
>
> The main features of this text are:
>
> - It has a **form** that consists of an **opening statement**, a **series of points** on both sides of the issue **supported by evidence**, and a **conclusion**. For example, the article makes the following point supported by evidence: '…the Count is based on a portrait of Vlad which has the inscription, "A wonderous…"'
>
> - It includes **phrases at the start of sentences** that signal which side of the issue is being written about. For example, 'Those who are convinced that Vlad is Bram Stoker's character…'
>
> - It uses **formal language,** written mainly in the **present tense**. For example, 'To draw a connection…*is* too far-fetched…'

1 Which paragraph tells the reader what the text is about?

2 a) Which paragraph gives a description of Vlad?

  b) Find three facts about him.

3 Identify one piece of evidence from paragraph 4 that supports the view that Vlad inspired Count Dracula.

4 The text is mainly written in the present tense. However, there are times when the past tense is used.

  a) Find two examples from two different paragraphs.

  b) Why has the past tense been used here?

5 Identify a phrase at the start of paragraph 5 that links it to the view expressed in paragraph 4.

Purpose

6 A discursive text presents views on a particular issue. What issue is being discussed in the article? Is it:
- whether Vlad was a vampire
- whether Bram Stoker's character of Dracula is based on Vlad
- whether Vlad was worse than Dracula?

In a discursive text, the **main issue** is usually stated somewhere in the first paragraph. However, this is not always the case. For example, in the article the main issue is stated in paragraph 4, in the form of a question: 'But how far did Bram Stoker base his vampire on Vlad?'

There are, however, **clues** that tell you what the main issue of the article is *before* you reach paragraph 4. For example, paragraph 1 is part of an introduction to the main issue. It is a quotation.

7 Who is the quote about and where does it come from?

8 Now reread paragraphs 2 and 3. At which point can you guess what the main issue of the article is? Write down the key words that tell you.

Reading for meaning

Discursive texts can be structured to present arguments in two ways:
- Some discursive accounts present one point of view followed by the opposite point of view. Then the next point is made followed by its opposite, and so on.
- Some discursive accounts present all the points for one viewpoint and then all the points for the opposite viewpoint.

9 Look again at the article. Which of these structures does this discursive text have?

10 You are going to search paragraphs 4 and 5 of the article for:
- the points that claim Dracula is based on Vlad
- the evidence given to back these points.

Look for key words and phrases and record your answers in a table like the one below. The first example has been completed for you.

Is Dracula based on Vlad?	
Points for	**Evidence**
Bram Stoker knew of Vlad's existence	Wikinson's book (mentions a warrior called Dracula)

11 When you have finished your table of 'Points for', draw up another table of 'Points against' Dracula being based on Vlad. Search paragraph 6 for the points against and the evidence given to back these points, then complete the table as you did for question 10.

Focus on: Useful phrases and connectives

There are many useful phrases that help to **introduce** and **link** the points being made in this discursive account. For example, lines 30–31 of the article state: '*They also claim* that the Count is based on a portrait of Vlad…'

12 Find another example of this kind of phrase in paragraph 5.

As you discovered in the 'Reading for meaning' section on page 22, discursive texts can present opposing viewpoints one after the other.

13 Complete the pairs of sentences below to give opposing viewpoints, using the information you recorded in the tables for questions 10 and 11. The first sentence has already been done for you, as an example.

> On the one hand, Bram Stoker knew of Vlad and his name 'Dracul'.
> On the other hand…
>
> One view is that…
> Alternatively…

Key Speaking and Listening

14 a) Working in groups, discuss how far you think Bram Stoker's *Dracula* is based on the life of Vlad the Impaler.

- To help you remember the viewpoints on both sides, refer to the information you recorded in the tables for questions 10 and 11.
- You will need to look carefully at the evidence. For example, we believe we know *where* Bram Stoker got the *name* 'Dracula' from, but we don't know how far the *character* of Dracula is based on Vlad?
- When discussing the evidence, use the phrases you have learnt in this section:
  - 'On the one hand…'
  - 'One view is that…'
  - 'On the other hand…'
  - 'Alternatively…'

b) At the end of your discussion, come to a group decision on the issue. Note down the main reasons for your group's decision.

c) Choose one member of your group to report your decision to another group.

4 Unit 1 Assignment: Gothic storyteller

Assessment Focus

> AF3 Organise and present whole texts effectively, sequencing and structuring information, ideas and events

You: are a storyteller.
Your task: to write a Gothic story or narrative for other students to read.

Stage 1

First choose a setting for your story from the following:

- a lonely graveyard
- a derelict theatre
- a disbanded fairground.

Describe the scene.

What time of day or night is it? What can you see and hear?

Use powerful description to give your setting a Gothic feel. Include:

- adjectives, for example:
  'It became a *devilish* shape in the *midnight* air...'
- adverbs, for example:
  'It crept *stealthily*...'

Then introduce your main character. In this story, you are going to be the main character, so you will need to write in the **first person** and use the **present tense**.

Points to remember

- Explain to your readers why you are in this setting. Is it by accident or on purpose?
- Do not give too much direct information about yourself – instead of *telling* the reader, *show* the reader. For example, instead of writing 'I was scared', you could write 'I felt the beads of sweat above my lip.'

Stage 2

Having created your setting and character, you now need to introduce the **problem** to overcome.
Introduce a 'presence' (for example, a ghost, vampire or unknown creature).
- Does it approach you? Is it in distress? Does it frighten you?
- Have you met this presence before?

Then think about the **crisis** of your story:
- What do you say to the presence?
- Do you have a clever way of tricking the presence?
- Do you have any supernatural powers? Do you need to use them?
- How do you attempt to resolve the crisis?

Finally, what will be the **ending** to your story?
- What happens to you? What happens to the presence?
- Did your plan to resolve the crisis work?
- Perhaps you received unexpected help. If you did, who or where did it come from?
- How do you feel about the way things end? Is the ending a happy or a sad one for you?

Stage 3

Now use your plan to write your Gothic story.

You can make the story flow better by:

- Using **connectives** to link ideas **within** paragraphs. For example, two things can happen at the same time:

  'As suddenly as it leapt forward, I heard the…'

- Using **connectives** to link ideas **across** paragraphs. For example, to shift to another scene you could begin a paragraph with:

  'Meanwhile, at the other side of the…'

- Using **conjunctions** to **lengthen your sentences** according to the Gothic style, for example, 'so' and 'but'.

Challenge

Look back at the descriptive language you used to describe a scene or events in your story.
- Can you make the language more Gothic in style by adding dramatic words or phrases?
- Can you make the speech more dramatic by changing the vocabulary or punctuation?

Unit 2 Tales retold

1 The Pig Scrolls

Aims

- Read an extract from a novel set in Ancient Greece
- Experiment with figurative language (Wr6)
- Develop an imaginative treatment of a traditional tale (Wr8)

This is an extract from *The Pig Scrolls* by Paul Shipton. It is set in Ancient Greece. Gryllus, who has been turned into a pig, is being taken on a journey by Sibyl, a prophetess. Their way through the mountains is blocked by a gigantic figure carved from the rock, with the body of a lion and the face of a human.

The Pig and the Sphinx

Sibyl was staring at the immense figure grimly. 'Er...Gryllus, I don't think a sculptor made this...' Her voice wobbled. 'I think that's the Sphinx. You know, the real Sphinx.'

'Not possible!' I scoffed. 'The Sphinx guarded the gates to Thebes, donkey's years ago! How could it be here? You're just being para–'

5   The Sphinx's great stone eyes opened. Slate-grey pupils levelled their steady gaze at us. If the cold look in those eyes was anything to go by, it wasn't about to win any Cuddliest Monster competitions. The rest of the stone creature's body didn't even twitch.

'–noid.'

10   Terror grabbed me by the roll of fat at the back of my neck and gave me a good shake. My bristles stood on end like a crack squad of Spartan soldiers on parade.

'Then again, you may have a point,' I said hurriedly, 'in which case, we really ought to be getting out of here.' I turned to go back the way we had come, but Sibyl blocked my path.

'We *can't* go back,' she said firmly. 'We can get past the Sphinx, I know we can. All we have to do is answer a riddle.'

She rested a hand on my back. Was she having a bash at a friendly gesture or making sure I didn't do a runner?

'Gryllus, you're good at riddles and stuff, aren't you?'

I could see where this was leading and I didn't like the scenery. I might not be one of those big-brained, book-stuffed boffins up at the Academy in Athens, but I have graduated with honours from the University of Life, which is where I learned the golden rule: *Never – and I Mean Never – Volunteer. For ANYTHING.*

'Not a chance!' I said.

Sibyl folded her arms crossly. 'But Gryllus, you told us you were brilliant at riddles! You said you'd got a million of them!'

True, I had heard a great many riddles during the long years of the Trojan War. I knew all the classics: 'How many Spartans does it take to screw in a torch-holder?' 'Why did the Hydra cross the road?' 'What time is it when Pluto, Lord of the Underworld, sits on your fence?' I probably did know a million of them.

'But what if today's question is number one million and one?' I whined. 'Like I said, NO CHANCE.'

There was a terrible sound like rock grinding and crumbling. In fact, it *was* rock grinding and crumbling as the Sphinx turned its tree-trunk sized neck to get a better look at us.

'I am the Questioner,' said the Sphinx, its voice stone on stone. 'Who shall be the Answerer?'

And without another word Sibyl took a step forwards.

At that moment, despite the many differences we'd had along the journey, despite all the squabbles and bickering, I couldn't help truly admiring the bravery of that simple act.

'He is,' said the prophetess, pointing at me.

Sphinx monster in the hills around the city of Thebes, who killed those who could not answer her riddles
paranoid unnecessarily fearful
Spartans people from Sparta, who were known for their military discipline
graduated with honours gained a good degree
Hydra a snake-like monster with many heads, killed by Heracles
prophetess a woman whose words are inspired by the gods

Tales retold

Key Reading

> **Narrative texts**
>
> This text is a **narrative**. Its **purpose** is to tell a story in an entertaining way.
>
> The main features of this text are:
>
> - It has a **structure** that includes an opening (**introduction**), a problem (**complication**), a dramatic moment when everything comes to a head (**crisis**) and an ending (**resolution**) when things are sorted out. For example, the crisis in the extract occurs when Sibyl names Gryllus as the Answerer.
> - It has **characters**, who the story is about. We often hear their words and thoughts.
> - It has a **narrator**, who tells the story in either the first person (I/we) or the third person (he/she/it). In this text, the narrator is one of the characters and tells the story in the first person, for example, 'I could see where this was leading…'
> - It uses **expressive** and **descriptive language**, for example, '"Not possible!" I scoffed.'
> - The characters' words are quoted using **direct speech**, for example, '"I am the Questioner," *said* the Sphinx…' ('said' is the reporting verb).

1 Who are the three characters in this extract? What is unusual about each of them?

2 What is the problem the main characters face in this episode?

3 At which point in the extract does the author remind us that the narrator is a pig?

4 a) 'Slate-grey pupils levelled their steady gaze at us' (lines 6–7). What effect does the author want to create with this description?

b) 'Scoffed' (line 4) is a stronger reporting verb than 'said'. Find one other reporting verb in the extract that you think is effective and explain why.

5 Who is speaking in line 10? How do you know?

Purpose

6 a) What is the main purpose of this extract? Choose from the following options and give a reason for your choice:
- To retell the myth of the Sphinx for modern readers.
- To make the reader laugh.
- To poke fun at a Greek myth.
- To move the plot of the book forward.

b) Which of the other purposes also fit this text? Point to evidence from the extract to support your answers.

Reading for meaning

7 a) At what point *exactly* does Gryllus realise that he is looking at the Sphinx?

b) How does the author make the Sphinx a frightening creature?

8 a) What word class do the following underlined words belong to?
- 'Sibyl was staring at the immense figure <u>grimly</u>.' (line 1)
- '"We *can't* go back," she said <u>firmly</u>.' (line 17)

b) What do words like this add to the dialogue?

One technique that the author uses for comic effect is a sudden change in tone or mood. For example:

> 'You're just being para–'
> The Sphinx's great stone eyes opened…
> '–noid.'

- Gryllus is confident that this isn't the Sphinx
- You can imagine Gryllus's face falling as he ends the word 'paranoid'

9 a) Analyse the final seven lines of the extract in the same way. How does the author build up one mood then suddenly dash it?

b) This technique is often used in comedy films and TV programmes. Discuss any examples that you have seen recently.

Exploring further

This 'version' of a Greek myth includes references to modern life. These are called **anachronisms**. They reflect something that could not have existed at the time, such as a Roman soldier wearing a watch.

10 Identify one anachronism and explain why the author included it.

11 Greek myths are usually narrated in serious, formal language. This version of a Greek myth uses a lot of informal language.

  a) Find three examples of informal language.

  b) What is the overall effect of such language?

Focus on: Imagery

This extract is not just a series of jokes. The author also tries to make the reader imagine the scene through his use of language.

One type of imagery the author uses is called a **simile**. A simile is a statement that compares one thing to another using the words 'like' or 'as'. For example:

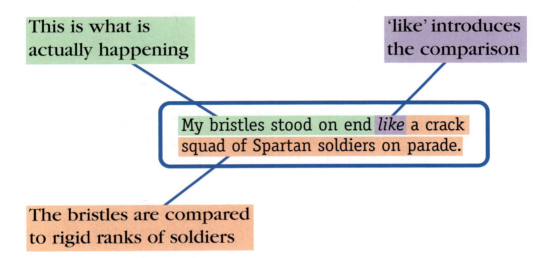

12 How effective is the simile in the example above? How does it help you to picture the scene in a particular way?

13 In pairs, complete the similes below. The images you use should make the reader see each scene in a special way. The first one has been done for you, as an example.

   a) The gymnast leapt through the air like a shooting star.
   b) Dark clouds gathered overhead like…
   c) Her teeth chattered with cold as if…
   d) He polished his motorbike like…
   e) She approached the water like…

Key Writing

14 Imagine that you are continuing the story of Gryllus and Sibyl. To make the riddle scene funny, try to make it sound like a TV game show in which Gryllus is a contestant and the Sphinx is the quizmaster. In the original story, the riddle was: 'What creature walks on four legs in the morning, two in the afternoon and three in the evening?'

a) Here are some of the features of a game show that you could refer to:
- finger on the buzzer
- phone a friend
- other contestants
- time pressure
- prizes
- weakest link.

Discuss these features with a partner. How could you use one or two of them?

b) Now role-play a dialogue with your partner. One of you will play Gryllus, the other will play the Sphinx. Think about these issues:
- Will you use the original riddle or change it?
- Will you bring Sibyl in somehow, perhaps as another contestant?
- Will the Sphinx break character to become the quizmaster or will Gryllus be the only one to make these game show references?

After your role play, jot down ideas for your narrative.

c) Now draft your episode together. You may want to begin like this:

'Here is your riddle, Answerer,' roared the Sphinx.

'Can't I have a starter for ten first?' I whimpered.

d) Try to include a simile in your episode. Remember that Gryllus has been turned into a pig. Does this suggest the kind of language that you could use?

2 Urban legends

- Read an explanation text about urban legends
- Remind yourself of the key features of explanation texts
- Explore how sentences are grouped together in paragraphs (S6)
- Write a short explanation (Wr11)

The following text is from the 'How Stuff Works' website.

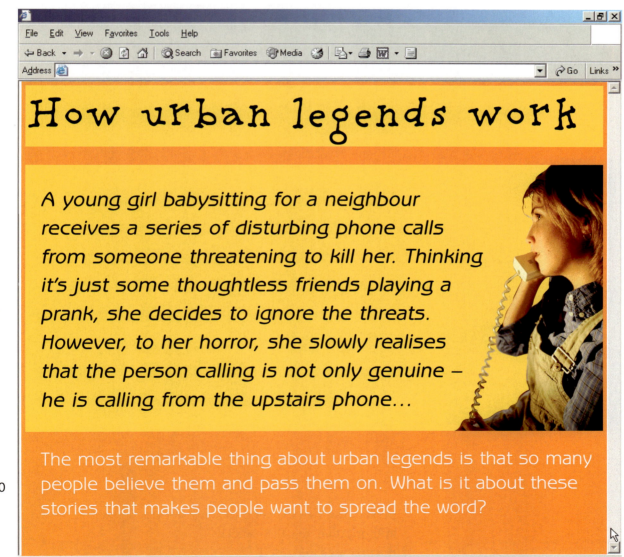

How urban legends work

A young girl babysitting for a neighbour receives a series of disturbing phone calls from someone threatening to kill her. Thinking it's just some thoughtless friends playing a prank, she decides to ignore the threats. However, to her horror, she slowly realises that the person calling is not only genuine – he is calling from the upstairs phone…

The most remarkable thing about urban legends is that so many people believe them and pass them on. What is it about these stories that makes people want to spread the word?

A lot of it has to do with the particular elements of the story. Many urban legends are about horrible crimes, contaminated foods or any number of occurrences that could affect a lot of people if they were true. If you hear such a story, and you believe it, you feel compelled to warn your friends and family.

Or a person might pass on information simply because it is funny or interesting. When you first hear the story, you are amazed that such a thing has occurred. When told correctly, a good urban legend will have you on the edge of your seat. It's human nature to want to spread this feeling to others, and be the one who's got everyone waiting to hear how the story turns out. Even if you hear it as a made-up joke, you might be tempted to personalise the tale by claiming it happened to a friend. Basically, people love to tell a good story.

Many people believe an urban legend must be true because it is reported by a newspaper, or other 'authoritative source'. The large number of Halloween stories (razors in apples, needles in candy) is an example of this. There are no documented cases of contamination of Halloween candy, but the media and police issue warnings year after year. Journalists, police officers and other authorities do get things wrong from time to time.

Another reason such stories get passed on is because the details make them seem real. You may have heard stories of children being kidnapped from a specific location, such as a local department store, or you may have heard about various gang initiations that occurred in a specific part of your town. Since you are familiar with the setting – you know it's a real place – the story sounds real. This level of detail also plays into your own fears and anxieties about what could happen to you in the places you visit regularly.

personalise make it refer to someone you know
authoritative reliable, official
documented recorded
initiation a ceremony that marks someone's entry into a club

Key Reading

Explanation texts

This text is an **explanation**. Its **purpose** is to help the reader understand how something works or why something has happened.

The main features of this text are:
- It has a series of **clear and logical steps**, for example, the first paragraph of the article makes it clear exactly what this text is setting out to explain.
- It uses **causal language** that shows how one thing causes another, for example, '*If* you hear such a story, *and* you believe it, you feel compelled to warn your friends and family.'
- It uses **formal** and **impersonal language**, for example, 'There are no documented cases of contamination of Halloween candy…'
- It is written mainly in the **present tense**, for example, 'Many urban legends *are* about horrible crimes…'

1 a) What is the first reason given in the article to explain how urban legends work?

  b) What is the second reason given?

2 The following sentence uses causal language:

> 'Or a person might pass on information simply because it is funny or interesting.'

  a) What is causing what to happen here?

  b) Identify the **causal connective** that shows it is a causal sentence.

3 a) What words or phrases make the following sentence formal?

> 'You might be tempted to personalise the tale.'

b) Rewrite this sentence in informal language.

4 a) Identify two verbs in the present tense in paragraph 1.
b) Why is the present tense usually used in explanation texts?

Purpose

5 What is the main purpose of this text? Choose from the following options, giving a reason for your choice:
- To explain what makes urban legends so gripping.
- To describe the different kinds of urban legends.
- To explain what makes people want to pass on urban legends.
- To explain why people should not believe in urban legends.

6 a) Which part of this text is *not* an explanation?
b) Why do you think it has been included here?

Reading for meaning

7 The main part of the article begins with a question (lines 9–10). An explanation text is supposed to give answers, not ask questions. What do you think the role of this question is?

The writer gives four reasons why so many people believe in urban legends. These are:

- Urban legends are often reported as true in newspapers and elsewhere.
- The stories contain things you want to warn your family and friends about.
- The stories seem real because of the local detail.
- The stories are so funny or amazing that you want them to be true.

8 a) Find the place where each of these reasons is discussed in the text.

b) How does the paragraphing help the reader to identify these reasons?

9 The writer uses causal connectives to highlight the link between cause and effect. For example, 'Another reason such stories get passed on is *because* the details make them seem real.'

a) Write down three examples of causal language in paragraph 3.

b) Underline the causal connective in each case.

> **Grammar for reading**
>
> A **connective** is a word or phrase that shows the connection between clauses or sentences. **Causal connectives** include 'because', 'if', 'when', 'since', 'so' and 'as'. For example, '*When* you turn the key in the lock, the door will open.'

> **Exploring further: Using the dash**
>
> **Dashes** (–) can sometimes be used in pairs to mark off a word, phrase or clause. It is an alternative to using brackets or commas for example, 'Since you are familiar with the setting – you know it's a real place – the story sounds real.' (lines 38–40)
>
> **10** Rewrite the following sentences to include dashes:
>
> **a)** Weigh the ingredients (cocoa, butter and sugar) and make the topping.
>
> **b)** 'That friend of yours, Ruth, called round earlier.'

Focus on: Grouping sentences into paragraphs

Sentences can be grouped into paragraphs in different ways. Look at the examples of paragraph openings below:

Turning the handle clockwise will lock the door. If you hear a double click, this means…

Topic sentence (or main point) of the paragraph

The rest of the paragraph **expands on the main point**

Topic sentence (or main point) of the paragraph

Every member of the team contributed to the victory. Beckham, for example…

The rest of the paragraph **gives examples**

Topic sentence (or main point) of the paragraph

The process is simple. First you phone 0118 345345. Then you…

The rest of the paragraph **gives a list in time order**

Topic sentence (or main point) of the paragraph

The process is simple. However, you may find that…

The rest of the paragraph **modifies the main point**

11 In pairs, analyse the article *How urban legends work*. For each of the five paragraphs identify:
- the purpose of the paragraph
- the topic sentence that makes the main point
- the role of the rest of the sentences in the paragraph. (You should refer to the four examples given on page 40.)

Draw up a chart to show your findings.

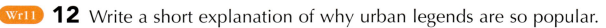

Key Writing

12 Write a short explanation of why urban legends are so popular.

a) First, brainstorm your ideas and add them to the spidergram below:

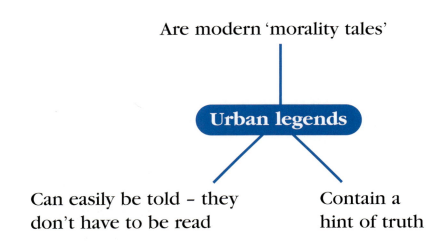

b) Now choose two or three of the reasons you have identified. You are going to draft a paragraph on each reason.
- State your main point in a **topic sentence** at the beginning of each paragraph.
- Group the rest of the sentences together in a logical way.
- Use **causal language** and **connectives** to guide the reader through your explanation. Causal connectives that you could use include 'because', 'when', 'if', 'since', 'as a result'.

The growth of a legend

Aims

- Read a magazine article about Robin Hood
- Remind yourself about the key features of analysis texts
- Examine the main uses of the comma (S3)
- Prepare a courtroom speech (S&L2)

The following text is adapted from a magazine article.

Analysis – Living Legends

Robin Hood: Prince of Thieves or Just a Petty Thief?

Robin Hood – we all know him, don't we? That heroic figure dressed in camouflage green, racing through Sherwood Forest with the gorgeous Marian by his side, stealing from the greedy, cowardly rich to give to the poor. He was the victim of a terrible injustice meted out by the evil Sheriff of Nottingham, and became an outlaw. But he was loved by ordinary people, as he only used violence against the 'baddies' and only killed in self-defence.

This is the story that we've all grown up with. But the legend of Robin Hood wasn't always like this. What makes legends so endlessly fascinating is that they adapt to the times: people come to have different interests and different beliefs, and the way they tell their favourite stories reflects these changes. So legends have a habit of changing as the years pass.

> His deeds are sung all over England…he was the prince of robbers, and the most humane. He permitted no harm to women, nor seized the goods of the poor, but helped them generously with what he took from abbots.
>
> *From a history of Britain, 1521*

> *He took Sir Guy's head by the hair,*
> *And stuck it on the end of his bow:*
> *'You have been a traitor all your life,*
> *To which there must come an end.'*
>
> *Robin pulled out an Irish knife,*
> *And slashed Sir Guy in the face,*
> *So that no one of a woman born*
> *Could tell who Sir Guy was.*
>
> *From a 15th-century poem*

Let's turn back the clock to the Middle Ages. In the original legend of Robin Hood – or at least all that we can glean from the poems and a fragment of a play that have survived – Robin helps a knight with a debt, then recovers the money by robbing the abbot who imposed the debt. In one poem Robin disguises himself as a potter and captures and kills the sheriff; in another, he kills Guy of Gisborne, a medieval 'bounty hunter' who is after him, savagely maltreating the corpse. In another, Robin himself is killed through the treachery of a cousin.

This hardly fits with the picture of the greenwood hero painted at the start! Robin is little more than a bold robber. He is also a small landowner, not a peasant or a knight – and certainly not a nobleman. He lives in the forest of Barnsdale in York, not Sherwood Forest in Nottingham, and there is no Maid Marian.

Over the centuries, the legend lost some of these features and gathered others. The Friar and Maid Marian, for example, were originally characters in the Morris dances. At some point around 1500 they entered the Robin Hood story, as Robin became celebrated as part of the spring festival. Later on he became a nobleman, the Earl of Huntingdon; later still he turned into the swashbuckling romantic hero that we see in the early films.

No doubt in the 22nd century the legend of Robin Hood will speak to us differently still.

meted out carried out
humane kind, civilised
glean pick up
bounty hunter someone paid money to capture or kill outlaws
greenwood a leafy or woody forest
swashbuckling adventurous, daredevil swordsman

Key Reading

> **Analysis texts**
>
> This text is an **analysis**. Its **purpose** is to study information or ideas closely.
>
> The main features of this text are:
> - It **states the issue** at the start then **explores** it by making points carefully; for example, the second paragraph makes the main point.
> - It uses **evidence** to support the points being made; for example, the quotes in the margin are evidence.
> - It uses **connectives** of cause and effect, and of time, for example, '*Later on* he became a nobleman…'
> - It is told mainly in the **present tense** (although it sometimes switches to the past tense to give background information), for example, 'In one poem Robin *disguises* himself as a potter…'

1 From the title, what aspect of Robin Hood is being analysed?

2 Paragraph 2 spells out the main point of this text.
   a) Which sentence in the paragraph summarises this point?
   b) What is the main purpose of paragraph 1?

3 The quotations in the margin relate to points being made in paragraphs 1 and 3. Identify which points they support.

4 a) 'So legends have a habit of changing as the years pass…' (lines 17–18).
   - How does this sentence relate to the ones before it?
   - What connective makes this clear to the reader?

   b) Find two connectives of time in paragraph 5.

5 When referring to events in stories, the present tense can be used instead of the past tense. Which tenses are used in paragraphs 1, 3, 4 and 5?

Purpose

6 What is the main purpose of this text?
- To tell the story of Robin Hood.
- To explore how and why the legend of Robin Hood has changed.
- To argue that Robin Hood was just a petty thief.
- To describe what historical sources say about Robin Hood.

Point to the evidence in the text that supports your answer.

Reading for meaning

7 Why is *Living Legends* such a good title for this article?

8 a) According to this text, the original legend of Robin Hood was different to the legend we know today. Make a note of some of these differences by drawing up a table like the one below.

Original legend	Legend as known today
Robin lives in Barnsdale, York.	He lives in Sherwood Forest, Nottingham.

b) According to the original legend, what kind of person was Robin Hood?

9 Look at the **first person** references in these sentences.
- 'This is the story that we've all grown up with' (line 11).
- 'Let's turn back the clock to the Middle Ages' (line 19).

Why do you think the author has used the first person at times in this article?

10 What does the writer mean by this last sentence?
'No doubt in the 22nd century the legend of Robin Hood will speak to us differently still.' (lines 39–40)

Focus on: The comma

The comma is a very common punctuation mark. However, it is also commonly misused. Here are some of the main uses of the comma:

- **To separate words or phrases in a list**, for example, '…stealing from the greedy, cowardly rich to give to the poor.' (Note that there does not need to be a comma after 'cowardly'. The last but one item in a list can go without a comma.)

- **To separate clauses in a sentence**, for example, 'But he was loved by ordinary people, as he only used violence…'

- **To mark off phrases in the middle of a sentence that give extra detail about something that has already been mentioned**, for example, 'Guy of Gisbourne, a medieval "bounty hunter", is savagely killed.' (Note that if you use the commas as 'hooks' to take the phrase out of the sentence, the sentence still makes sense.)

11 Using the information above, write out these sentences and put in the missing commas.

   a) Robin's closest companions were Little John Maid Marian Alan a Dale and Will Scarlet.

   b) Drawing an arrow from his quiver Robin took aim and fired.

   c) Little John a giant of a man crushed the knight with one blow.

   d) As soon as he had entered the castle he took off his disguise.

   e) Robin later the Earl of Huntingdon became the greenwood hero.

Exploring further: When commas are not needed

However long the sentence is, you should never put a comma between the subject and the verb. For example:

Subject (noun phrase) Verb

This morning's exploration of the effect of tourism on African countries will have to be postponed until next week.

12 Decide if this sentence needs any commas:
'The least-liked and most notorious character in the Robin Hood legend turns out to be not so bad.'

Key Speaking and Listening

13 Robin Hood is in court. The charge against him is that he is no more than a common thief. Working in pairs, decide whether you will **defend** Robin or **prosecute** him.

a) First of all, discuss the facts that will support your case. Make brief notes on the following:
- Robin's main aims as an outlaw
- How he treated people
- What crimes he committed as an outlaw
- Who supported him, who opposed him, and why
- What his attitude towards justice and authority was
- What his personal qualities, skills and background were.

In each case, be prepared to back up your judgement with evidence. Draw on points made in the article and your own knowledge of the Robin Hood legend.

b) Next, prepare your speech for court. Use your notes as your main points and include the following features of analysis:
- A piece of evidence to back up each point.
- Connectives to show the cause and effect of each view offered.
- Connectives to contrast different views you put forward.

c) Decide who will deliver the speech and who will be on hand to help provide or read out evidence. Practise delivering the speech and make changes to improve it. Remember that your speech must **persuade the court** as well as **analyse the evidence**, so vary your pace and tone for effect. Be prepared to deliver it to the court.

④ Unit 2 Assignment: The detective

Assessment Focus

▸ AF3 Organise and present whole texts effectively, sequencing and structuring information, ideas and events

> **You:** are Shylock Holmes, a literary detective.
> **Your task:** to analyse two story openings. You must prove which is an urban legend and which is a straight story. You will use your skills in writing an analysis.

Stage 1

Read the two story openings (**A** and **B**) carefully. Then read the 'feature' panels on page 50. Discuss with a partner which opening is from the urban legend and which is from the straight story. Can you identify all the characteristic features of each type of story?

Story opening A

It was the same most evenings. Sam picked up Becky and drove his wreck to the parking area two miles outside town. There they could play the car radio full blast; they could hang out on their own.

It was already half dark when they heard the local news: '…escaped from Locksley Prison…convicted for murder…'

Story opening B

Did you hear what happened to this couple? They're friends of someone Jack knows.

They're on a date, and they've driven out to a quiet country road. They hear this report on the local radio about an escaped killer with a hooked hand…

Features of a straight story:
- Characters who you can became interested in
- Direct speech, in quote marks
- Imaginative use of language
- Narrative with lots of detail
- Formal language
- Past tense more common.

Features of an urban legend:
- 'Cardboard' characters
- Mostly narrative, little direct speech
- Plain language, reflecting speech
- Simple narrative, including only basic facts
- Informal language
- Present tense commonly used.

Stage 2

On your own, jot down at least eight points that help to prove your theory. Write them in **note form** and put the **evidence** next to them. For example:

Characters are named (in story A) – as in straight stories. Evidence: 'Sam picked up Becky.'

Stage 3

Now plan your report. Organise your notes into four paragraphs:
- **Paragraph 1**: state the problem clearly.
- **Paragraph 2**: summarise the features that make urban legends different from straight stories.
- **Paragraph 3**: show what kind of text story A is.
- **Paragraph 4**: show what kind of text story B is.

Stage 4

Now write your report. Remember:

- Begin each paragraph with a sentence stating the main point.
- Use causal connectives to make your analysis clear, for example, 'because', 'in effect'.
- Use connectives to contrast two different views of evidence, for example, 'but', 'however'.
- Use the present tense.
- Use phrases to integrate pieces of evidence, such as 'for example…', 'as we can see…' and 'in paragraph 1 we read…'

Challenge

Add a **conclusion** to your report.

- It should summarise your findings, perhaps by referring back to the introduction.
- It could highlight one or two of your key pieces of evidence as the most important.

Unit 3 Magic and illusion

1 The Lord of the Rings

Aims

- Read an extract from a narrative
- Learn the difference between literal and inferred meaning (R7)
- Learn what symbols mean in a narrative and create your own symbol (W11)
- Learn how the writer can break the mood
- Learn how verse can feature in a narrative

In this extract from early in *The Lord of the Rings* by J.R.R. Tolkien, the wizard Gandalf has paid Frodo an important visit. Something spectacular is about to happen…

An ancient secret

'Give me the ring for a moment.'

Frodo took it from his breeches-pocket, where it was clasped to a chain that hung from his belt. He unfastened it and handed it slowly to the wizard. It felt suddenly very heavy, as if either it or Frodo himself was in some way reluctant for Gandalf to touch it.

Gandalf held it up. It looked to be made of pure and solid gold. 'Can you see any markings on it?' he asked.

'No,' said Frodo. 'There are none. It is quite plain, and it never shows a scratch or sign of wear.'

'Well then, look!' To Frodo's astonishment and distress the wizard threw it suddenly into the middle of a glowing corner of the fire. Frodo gave a cry and groped for the tongs; but Gandalf held him back.

15 'Wait!' he said in a commanding voice, giving Frodo a quick look from under his bristling brows.

No apparent change came over the ring. After a while Gandalf got up, closed the shutters outside the window, and drew the curtains. The room became dark and silent, though the clack of
20 Sam's shears, now nearer to the windows, could still be heard faintly from the garden. For a moment the wizard stood looking at the fire, then he stooped and removed the ring to the hearth with the tongs, and at once picked it up. Frodo gasped.

'It is quite cool,' said Gandalf, 'Take it!' Frodo received it on
25 his shrinking palm: it seemed to have become thicker and heavier than ever.

'Hold it up!' said Gandalf, 'And look closely!'

As Frodo did so, he now saw fine lines, finer than the finest pen-strokes, running along the ring, outside and inside: lines of
30 fire that seemed to form the letters of a flowing script. They shone piercingly bright, and yet remote, as if out of a great depth.

'I cannot read the fiery letters,' said Frodo in a quavering voice.

'No,' said Gandalf, 'but I can. The letters are Elvish, of an ancient mode, but the language is that of Mordor, which I will not utter here. But this in the Common Tongue is what is said,
35 close enough:

One Ring to rule them all, One Ring to find them,
One Ring to bring them all and in the darkness bind them.'

---

breeches trousers
shears large garden scissors
hearth fireside
tongs tool used for lifting coals from the fire
mode style

Key Reading

Narrative texts

This text is an extract from a **narrative**. Its **purpose** is to tell a story in an entertaining way.

The main features of this text are:

- It has a **structure** that includes an opening (**introduction**), a problem (**complication**), a dramatic moment when everything comes to a head (**crisis**) and an ending (**resolution**) when things are sorted out. *The Lord of the Rings* is an **epic narrative**. There are brave deeds and adventures and many complications and crises before the long story comes to an end.

- It has **characters**, who the story is about. We often hear their words and thoughts. In an epic narrative the main character is often an ordinary person who is called upon to carry out a special task, for example, in *The Lord of the Rings,* the main character is Frodo Baggins. Since *The Lord of the Rings* is a fantasy novel, not all the characters are human. However, we still hear their words and thoughts.

- It has a **narrator**, who tells the story in either the first person (I/we) or the third person (he/she/it). The narrator of an epic narrative usually tells the story in the third person, for example, '…then *he* stooped and removed the ring…'

- It features **powerful words** so that the narrative is interesting to read or listen to, for example, 'They shone *piercingly bright*, and yet *remote*, as if out of a great depth.'

1 What is the most important thing that happens in this extract from *The Lord of the Rings*?

2 Who is the wise character in the extract? How can you tell?

3 Find another example in paragraph 1 that shows this is a third person narrative.

4 Find a powerful phrase that describes the room where Gandalf and Frodo meet.

5 What feeling are you left with at the end of the extract?

Purpose

The purpose of a narrative is to entertain us.
Sometimes the writer will do this by making us curious.

6 By the end of this extract, what do you want to know more about?

Reading for meaning

A text can be read in different ways to get different information. Remember that:

- **literal meaning** is information that the reader can be certain of
- **inferred meaning** is information that is hidden – the reader has to work out or *infer* what is meant.

The Lord of the Rings contains both kinds of meaning.

7 Find an example of literal meaning in paragraph 1.

In paragraph 2 of the extract, the ring is described in the following way:

> It felt suddenly very heavy, as if either *it* or Frodo himself *was in some way reluctant* for Gandalf to touch it.

This suggests the ring 'thinks' or has feelings. From this you can *infer* that the ring has some kind of power

Magic and illusion

8 a) Read the passage below, paying particular attention to the numbered parts.

> 1 → No apparent change came over the ring. After a while *Gandalf got up*, closed the shutters outside ← 2
> the window, and *drew the curtains. The room*
> 3 → *became dark and silent*, though the clack of Sam's shears, now nearer to the windows, could still be heard faintly from the garden. For a moment the wizard stood looking at the fire, then he stooped and *removed the ring to the hearth with the tongs,* ← 4
> and at once picked it up. *Frodo gasped.* ← 5

R7

b) Decide which numbered parts have literal meanings and which have inferred meanings.

c) Complete a chart like the one below for the five numbered parts. Tick the second or third column to show whether the meaning is literal or inferred. If the meaning is inferred, write its hidden meaning in the last column.

Numbered part	Literal meaning	Inferred meaning	Hidden meaning

Exploring further: Breaking the mood

Sometimes writers introduce an ordinary event into a tense part of the story. This breaks the mood for a moment before leading into an even more exciting part.

9 Study the paragraph in question 8 again. Find the lines that tell you what Sam is doing. How do these break the mood?

Focus on: Reading the signs

At a simple level, a **sign** or **symbol** is a picture or expression that means something else, for example, a frown means displeasure; a green traffic light means 'go'.

Symbols are also found in narratives. In *The Lord of the Rings* the ring is a symbol, although its meaning is harder to work out. It has more than one meaning, but the reader does not discover all of these until the end of the story. However, it is possible to pick up some clues to its meaning from the extract.

For example, in the 'Reading for meaning' section on page 55, it was inferred that the ring had some kind of power. This meaning is recorded in the table below.

The ring as a symbol	
Information in extract	**Meaning that can be inferred**
Very heavy, as if reluctant for Gandalf to touch it.	The ring seems to think or feel; has some kind of power.
Pure solid gold.	
No obvious markings on it.	
Cool when heated by fire.	
Becomes heavier when heated.	
Ancient language written in fire revealed.	

W11 **10 a)** The table above lists further information from the extract about the ring. Complete the table by writing what you infer from each piece of information.

b) Summarise what the ring could symbolise from the information you have collected in the table.

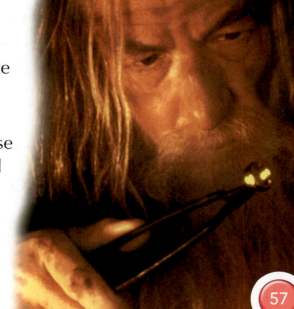

Exploring further: Rhymes and riddles

Traditional fantasy fiction, such as folk tales, often contains riddles in verse that are linked to magic.

11 a) Read the rhyming verse at the end of the extract. It gives information about the power of the ring. What is the most important thing that you infer from it?

b) How does the rhyme emphasise this message?

Key Writing

12 a) You are going to create your own symbol. You could start with one of the ideas in the table below.

Symbol	Features	Hidden meaning
Key	Can lock and unlock doors	Imprisonment
Book	Can speak	Knowledge
Crown	Can glow in the dark	Protection

b) Your symbol will have a number of features. List them in a similar table. To decide what these features are, ask yourself the following questions:
- What is it made of?
- What can it do?
- What are its weaknesses?
- What are its strengths?

c) Choose the most important hidden meaning for your symbol and explain it to a partner.

2 The Nose

Aims

- Read the poem, *The Nose*
- Learn about the style and form of the poem (R10)
- Identify different kinds of images in the poem
- Learn about run-on lines
- Write your own poem (Wr7)

This poem by Iain Crichton-Smith is written in a fantasy-like style.

The Nose
(after Gogul)

The nose went away by itself
in the early morning
while its owner was asleep.
It walked along the road
5   sniffing at everything.

It thought: I have a personality of my own.
Why should I be attached to a body?
I haven't been allowed to flower.
So much of me has been wasted.

10   And it felt wholly free.
It almost began to dance
The world was so full of scents
it had had no time to notice,

15 when it was attached to a face
    weeping, being blown,
    catching all sorts of germs
    and changing colour.

    But now it was quite at ease
    bowling merrily along
20 like a hoop or a wheel,
    a factory packed with scent.

    And all would have been well
    but that, round about evening,
    having no eyes for guides,
25 it staggered into the path
    of a mouth, and it was gobbled
    rapidly like a sausage
    and chewed by great sour teeth –
    and that was how it died.

Gogul Reference to Nikolai Gogul (1809–1852), a Russian writer. He wrote a story called The Nose, in which a man loses his nose

Key Reading

Poetry

This text is a **poem**. Its **purpose** is to explore feelings and ideas.

A poem is made up of **images**, **rhythm** and **form**.
- The **images** are the pictures made by the words.
- The **rhythm** is like the beat in music.
- The **form** is the framework or pattern of the poem. Poems are written in **lines** not sentences.

Other important features of poems:
- Some poems **rhyme**, for example, the words 'dream' and 'seem' rhyme.
- Some poems are **free verse**. They have lines of different lengths with different rhythms. (Some free verse contains rhyme.)

1 How does the nose feel about its face?

2 a) Over what time period does the story take place?

   b) What happens to the nose by the end of the poem?

3 How would you describe this poem? Choose from the following options (you can choose more than one answer):
   - It is a poem that tells a story.
   - It is a free verse poem.
   - It is a poem with a regular beat or rhythm.

4 Can you find any rhymes in the poem?

5 Which do you think is the most memorable image in the poem?

Purpose

6 a) What do you think is the **main reason** why this poem was written? Choose from the following options:
   - To tell a story.
   - To make the reader laugh.
   - To make the reader sad or thoughtful.
   - To make the writer laugh.

   b) Compare your answer with that of a partner.

Magic and illusion

Reading for meaning

The poem has the style of a simple narrative. It is also a fantasy. Like most fantasies it is similar to a traditional folk tale. It could almost begin, 'Once upon a time there was a nose…' However, it also has differences.

R10

7 a) Read this list of features often found in folk tales.

Features of the folk tale:
- strange characters or creatures
- strange events
- a journey.

The main character:
- seeks adventure
- meets danger
- may escape by magic
- outwits enemies
- may be freed from a spell
- triumphs in the end.

b) Now draw up a chart like the one below.
- In column 1, write down those features that *The Nose* shares with a folk tale.
- In column 2, write down those features that *The Nose* does *not* share with a folk tale.

Features shared with a folk tale	Features not shared with a folk tale

c) In your view, what is the most important way in which *The Nose* differs from a folk tale?

Exploring further

All folk tales, however simple, contain a lesson about life. Perhaps this is also true of *The Nose*.

8 With a partner, discuss whether you think the nose was right to leave its face. The obvious answer seems to be 'no' since it was gobbled up by a mouth… but is it?

9 In pairs, answer these questions using evidence from the poem:

   a) What was life like for the nose when it was attached to the face?

   b) Was there any benefit in the nose leaving the face?

   Come to an agreement and then report back to another pair in the class.

Focus on: Building images

Although *The Nose* is told like a simple folk tale, it also contains unusual images. Most appeal to the sense of sight. For example, the poem opens with:

> The nose went away by itself
> in the early morning
> while its owner was asleep.

10 a) The image that follows in the first verse appeals to a different sense. What is it?

   b) Why would you expect this poem to contain images that appeal to this particular sense?

   c) Find another example of an image appealing to this sense in verse 3.

11 A **simile** compares one thing with another using 'like' or 'as'. It is used to make an image more vivid.

Identify the two similes in the poem. Write them down using quotation marks and note which verse they are in.

12 a) Reread verse 6 where the mouth appears. Make a spidergram of the mouth's special features, like this:

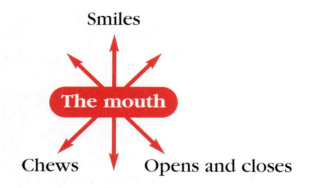

b) Choose the most interesting features from your spidergram and write two similes for the mouth. For example, 'The mouth grinned like a trap shut tight.'

13 Another way of developing an image is to use a **metaphor**. Unlike a simile, a metaphor does not compare one thing with another, but describes it as *being* another.

a) Find the metaphor for the nose in the poem.

b) Create your own metaphor for the mouth, based on another feature from your spidergram. For example, 'A chewing monstrous creature, the mouth…'

Exploring further: Run-on lines

The Nose is written in free verse so it has no regular rhythm or beat. In some lines there is also **no pause at the end**. This means the idea is carried on from one line to the next. For example:

> when it was attached to a face — **No pause**
> weeping, being blown… — **Line runs on**

In addition, when the poem is read aloud it sounds more like speech than, for example, the regular beat of a song or a ballad.

14 Find three more examples of run-on lines in the poem.

Key Writing

 15 Write a free verse poem based on *The Nose* about the mouth that gobbles up the nose.

a) Begin by making a short story plan. Use *The Nose* as a model. Consider:
- where the mouth comes from
- what problem it encounters
- what danger it is in
- how the story ends.

b) Next, give your poem some structure. If you find it helpful, begin by writing in sentences that you can then change or break up into the lines of your poem. For example:

> **Sentence:** Once upon a time there was a mouth. — **Words left out**
> **Lines:**
> Once
> there was a mouth. — **Lines of different lengths**

c) Try to use some of the similes and metaphors you created in questions 12 and 13 to make the images in your poem more vivid.

3 Trick of the mind

Aims

- Read a series of explanations
- Learn how to separate description from explanation (R4)
- Learn the difference between the active and the passive

Derren Brown is a magician. Here he explains some of the secrets of the tricks shown in his television series.

Derren Brown plays tricks

Most people can be wrong-footed if you behave in a way that's unexpected. Once I was walking along a street when a man said threateningly: 'What are you looking at?' I answered a completely different question, saying: 'The wall outside my house is not 4ft high.' He looked dumbfounded and repeated his question. I again gave a completely irrelevant answer, saying: 'I used to live in Spain.' He was so perplexed by my failure to respond in the way he'd anticipated that he gave up and ran off.

The abandoned wallet

When I leave a cash-filled wallet on the pavement in a busy street all day, I am playing with people's perceptions. By drawing a line around it, I disconcert them even more by making it look 'official'.

No one touches the wallet because they think it's too weird or perhaps some sort of trap. People know that lines are drawn round the shape of the body if someone has died in suspicious circumstances, so that makes them feel the wallet has been put there by the authorities. The line makes it clear that it's not lying there by accident.

I don't think the trick would work without the line around the wallet. It makes the object look surreal, as though it has been put there for some unknown purpose...

The aim of this trick of the mind is to make people feel so weird about picking up the wallet that they would rather play safe and not touch it. And it works!

Are you feeling sleepy?

All through the series, people mysteriously fall asleep in public phone boxes. Have they fallen prey to a disease or am I carrying out some trick of the mind on the other end of the line? There are two factors at work here.

First, the group of people subjected to the stunt are particularly suggestible. I know this simply because they chose to answer a public phone that happened to be ringing as they walked past. Most people would ignore it, assuming it was nothing to do with them.

Secondly, once the person answers, I immediately bombard them with a rapid set of confusing instructions and facts. I do this for several minutes without giving give them a break, then follow it by telling them to fall asleep. As seen on the shows, this works.

---

wrong-footed put (someone) in a difficult situation
dumbfounded amazed
disconcert upset, puzzle
surreal dreamlike, unreal
suggestible easily influenced by suggestion
bombard attack

Magic and illusion

Key Reading

Explanation texts

This text is mainly an **explanation** but it also contains some **description**. Its **purpose** is to explain how something might work and why things happen.

The main features of this text are:
- It has a series of **clear and logical steps**, for example, in the second paragraph of the article Derren Brown writes: 'By drawing a line around it, I disconcert them even more…' This makes the first point of 'The abandoned wallet'.
- When giving an explanation it is written in the **present tense**, for example, 'I *am playing* with people's perceptions…'
- When describing how something has happened it is written in the **past tense**, for example: 'Once I *was walking* along a street when a man *said* threateningly…'
- It uses **causal language** to show how one thing causes another, for example, 'No one touches the wallet *because*…'
- It uses **subheadings** when discussing different explanations. This makes the text easier to read.

1 What kind of things does Derren Brown explain in the text?

2 More than one tense is used in paragraph 1. Find an example of something written using:

   a) the present tense

   b) the past tense.

3 What two subheadings are used in the article?

4 Find another example of causal language in the second paragraph of the section 'The abandoned wallet'.

Purpose

5 a) What is Derren Brown trying to do in this text? Choose from the following options:
- To demonstrate magic tricks.
- To show that people are easily fooled.
- To tell the reader why the tricks work.

b) Which other purpose from the list is also true of the text?

Reading for meaning

Explanation texts can describe and explain, but not at the same time. For example, in paragraph 1 of the text the writer *describes* an incident:

> Man confronts Derren Brown in street → Derren Brown talks nonsense → Man runs away.

In the last sentence of paragraph 1, however, the writer *explains* why the man ran away:

> He was so perplexed by my failure to respond in the way he'd anticipated that he gave up and ran off.

You could reword the explanation in note form in the following ways:

> Derren Brown confused the man *so* the man ran away.

> The man ran away *because* Derren Brown confused him.

Remember, the connectives 'so' and 'because' show the link between cause and effect.

R3

6 Working in groups, study paragraphs 1 and 2 of the section 'The abandoned wallet'.

  a) Discuss what the events are. One person should scan the two paragraphs to gain this information.

  b) Another group member then sums up the events in note form, as shown in the two examples on page 69. You should agree as a group how the notes are worded.

7 a) As a group, read through your summary of events from question 6. Ask the question, 'Why did people avoid the wallet?'

  b) In the article, Derren Brown gives several reasons why people avoided the wallet. Find these reasons and discuss them as a group. In your discussion, use expressions such as 'What about…?' and 'Does this mean...?' to help you.

Wr11

  c) Reword Derren Brown's explanations to show the cause and effect, using the connectives 'so' or 'because'. For example:

  'The line around the wallet makes it look official so...'

  d) Choose a group member to report back with your summaries. Keep your notes safe since you will use them for your written work in question 11.

8 a) Still in your group, read the section 'Are you feeling sleepy?' Work through the paragraphs, recording the events as you did for question 6.

  b) No clear explanation is given for why the people fell asleep. However, there are clues in the text.
  - Find key words that help to explain how the trick works. For example, 'There are two factors at work here…'
  - Decide what the explanation might be and record your answer using the causal connectives 'so' and 'because'.

  c) Choose a group member to report what you have found to another group.

9 On your own, decide what the main difference is between describing and explaining. Write down your answer in two sentences.

Focus on: The active and the passive

When Derren Brown *describes* his tricks, he often writes in the **active tense**. At such times he talks directly to the audience in an informal, chatty way. For example:

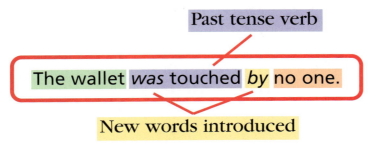

However, when Derren Brown *explains* the reasons why things happen, he sometimes writes in the **passive tense**. When using the passive tense, the writing is more formal, for example, the sentence 'No one touches the wallet' could be written in the passive like this:

10 Change the following sentences from the passive to the active:

a) Another trick was performed by Derren Brown.

b) They were all fooled by a fake séance.

c) The audience were convinced by the magic stunt.

Key Writing

11 Think back to the group work you did for questions 6 and 7. You are now going to rewrite 'The abandoned wallet' section in your own words from memory.

- You will need to describe the trick and explain how it works.
- Refer to your notes from questions 6 and 7 on the events and reasons behind the trick.
- Use **causal language** and **connectives** to show how the cause and effect are linked in your explanation.
- Include the **passive** in some of your explanation sentences.

Unit 3 Assignment: The magician

Assessment Focus

- AF5 Vary sentences for clarity, purpose and effect

You: are a magician with x-ray eyes.
Your task: to write an explanation showing how a conjuring trick works.

Stage 1

Read the description of the conjuring trick below.

> Ask six members of the audience to write a word on a sheet of paper, fold it in half, place it an envelope and seal it.
>
> 'With my x-ray eyes,' you say, 'I will read every word correctly!'
>
> To demonstrate your skill, pick up an envelope, show that your hands and sleeves are free, and with a flourish, lift the envelope to your x-ray eyes. Slowly spell out the word. Someone in the audience gasps. You have spelled out *their* word.
>
> Pick up the next envelope. The same thing happens – and you work through each envelope spelling out each correct word.

Stage 2

Here are notes that explain the trick. Working with a partner, read through the notes and ensure that you understand them.

- You have an accomplice in the audience.
- You agree on a word (for example, 'cabbage'.)
- Accomplice is given an envelope and writes down 'cabbage.'
- You collect the envelopes.
- Accomplice's envelope placed at bottom of pile.
- You pick up top envelope.
- Spell out 'cabbage'.
- Accomplice confirms the word and appears amazed.
- You open envelope, read aloud false word: 'cabbage'. But to yourself you read real word (for example, 'goat').
- You pick up another envelope.
- Spell out 'goat'.
- Confirmed by member of audience who wrote the word 'goat'.
- You open envelope, read aloud false word: 'goat'. But to yourself you read real word...
- And so on to the last envelope.

Stage 3

Write up the notes from Stage 2 as an explanation.

- Make a series of clear points in your explanation. For example, 'first...', 'then...', 'next...'
- Use the first person (I) when referring to yourself. (Remember, you are the magician.) Use the first person (we) when referring to yourself and your accomplice.
- Write in the present tense.
- Use causal connectives such as 'so' and 'because' to give reasons why the trick works.

Remember:
Be careful not to write in the same style as the notes (each line of the notes reads in the same way). To avoid this and to make your explanation more interesting, you should vary your sentences. For example, use the active and the passive:

Active: 'I give my accomplice an envelope.'

Passive: 'An envelope is given to my accomplice.'

Unit 4 Destructive nature

1 Twister!

Aims

- Read an information text about tornadoes
- Examine the layout of a text
- Use the library and ICT to research and present information (R2)
- Write an information text (Wr10)

This text is from an information book for young people.

TORNADO ALLEY

Tornadoes happen all over the world and are most common in North America, Europe, East Asia and Australia. In the United States, about 800 tornadoes are reported every year and around 70 people are killed. Waves of warm, moist air from the Gulf of Mexico often clash with cooler, dry winds
5 from the northern states of Canada and the Rocky Mountains. This clash leads to many tornadoes forming along a wide stretch of country through the states of Texas, Oklahoma, Kansas and Nebraska, which has earned the region the nickname of 'tornado alley'. Most of the region's twisters occur in April, May and June, and they account for over a third of all US tornadoes.
10 They usually occur during the afternoon or early evening, but there have been some night-time tornadoes. Florida is also often hit by tornadoes.

Twister!

It is no good trying to simply outrun a tornado – it will almost certainly catch up with you. Anyone outside when a tornado approaches should try and move quickly away from the storm's path. If there is no time to escape the tornado's path, it is best to lie flat in the nearest ditch. Some houses in high-risk areas have an underground storm cellar for protection.

The Alley

An average of 125 tornadoes are reported in Texas every year, with over 50 in Oklahoma, 48 in Kansas and 38 in Nebraska. About ten people are killed by twisters every year in Texas alone. This map shows how tornadoes are swept in by warm winds off the Gulf of Mexico.

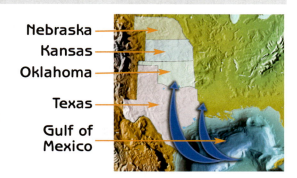

Toto

The National Severe Storms Laboratory is situated right in the middle of high-risk 'tornado alley' in Oklahoma. Scientists there have developed a barrel of instruments that can be dropped in a tornado's path to measure its temperature, air pressure, wind speed and direction. They call this the Totable Tornado Observatory – TOTO for short, after the name of the dog in The Wonderful Wizard of Oz. TOTO weighs 180kg (397lbs) and is transported on the back of a special pick-up lorry.

Bermuda Triangle

In the seas of the Atlantic Ocean between Bermuda, Florida and Puerto Rico, there is a mysterious area known as the Bermuda Triangle. Many ships and planes have disappeared here without trace. In 1945 a squadron of five US planes on a training mission vanished at the same time, and a search plane sent out to look for them also went missing. More than 50 ships are said to have disappeared in the region. One theory is that they were lost in storms, especially waterspouts, in that area.

Texan Twister

Texas suffers more tornadoes than any other state in the USA. On 11 May 1953, a single tornado hit Waco in central Texas, just 300 km (186 miles) from the coast of the Gulf of Mexico, killing 114 people. The worst US tragedy happened in 1925, when a group of tornadoes hit the states of Missouri, Illinois and Indiana, killing a total of 689 people.

---

storm cellar underground shelter, often equipped with supplies and first aid equipment
squadron unit in the Air Force of two or more flights of aircraft

Destructive nature

Key Reading

Information texts

This text is mainly an **information** text. Its **purpose** is to give clear information about a topic.

The main features of this text are:

- It is written in the **present tense** when telling things as they are, for example, '800 tornadoes *are* reported every year…'
- It is written in the **past tense** when providing details of past events, for example, 'The worst US tragedy *happened* in 1925…'
- The **layout of the text** includes photographs and maps to attract the reader's attention and present information visually.
- It uses **headings** and **subheadings** to make it easier to find information, for example, information on tornadoes in Texas is given under the subheading 'Texan Twister'.
- It includes both **general information** and **specific facts**, often using technical language, for example:
  General fact: 'Tornadoes happen all over the world…'
  Specific fact: '[scientific instruments] measure… temperature, air pressure, wind speed and direction.'

1 Find three examples of the present tense in the extract.

2 When is the extract written in the past tense and why? Find an example.

3 Identify two specific facts, using technical language.

4 a) What kinds of visual information are included in the text? Find two different examples.

  b) What part of the text does each illustration refer to? Write down the subheadings.

Purpose

Although the main purpose of this text is to give information on tornadoes, it also contains an explanation.

5 a) Where does the explanation begin in paragraph 1?

b) What is it about? Write down the words that tell you.

Reading for meaning

The layout of an information text helps to guide the reader. It is not simply there to look attractive – it allows the reader to **browse** the page. You do not need to begin at the beginning and read each paragraph. Instead, you can easily select the parts you want to read.

6 Look at the text and note as many features as you can that aid reading. Think about:
- the headings
- the font or typeface
- the different kinds of visual information.

7 a) Read the following information again. It contains several facts.

> ### The Alley
> An average of 125 tornadoes are reported in Texas every year, with over 50 in Oklahoma, 48 in Kansas and 38 in Nebraska. About ten people are killed by twisters every year in Texas alone.

b) Work out a way of laying out this information as a simple chart.

c) What heading will you give your chart?

d) What information is missing from the above extract that would complete your chart?

8 a) Find the paragraph in the text which offers three pieces of advice to someone caught in the path of a tornado.

b) Rewrite the advice to make it sound more urgent. You will need to change the layout, language and punctuation.
The rewriting has been started for you below. Note the changes and then complete the advice.

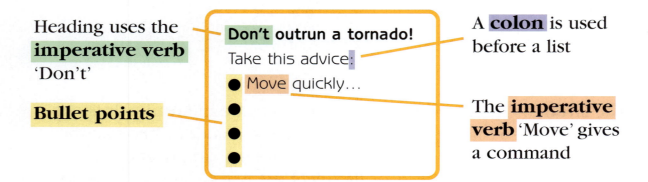

> ### Exploring further: Providing details
>
> Details or examples often follow a general comment in an information text. This can happen within a sentence or a paragraph. For example:
>
> General comment　　　　　　　　　　　　　　Details
>
> > Tornadoes happen all over the world and are most common in North America, Europe, East Asia and Australia.
>
> **9** Find another example of this technique.

Focus on: Carrying out research

You can find more information about tornadoes by researching in books or through databases. A **database** is a way of storing facts in a list or table on a computer.

Which method would give you the best information? This depends on what you want to know. For example, if you want specific facts about tornadoes, a database would be the best method. You can find this type of information on CD-ROMs or websites.

R2 **10 a)** Read the section 'Texan Twister' again. Then, with your teacher's guidance, carry out ICT research using suitable databases to find out the following information about tornadoes in Texas:

- some of the most severe tornadoes
- when these took place
- the wind speed of the tornadoes
- the damage to homes and crops.

Use a search engine effectively to help you. Remember to include key words in each search question. For example, if you leave out the word 'Texas' you will not get the information you want.

b) Create a document of the most interesting facts under sub-headings. You will use these in question 13.

Destructive nature

Exploring further: Book research tips

Using books for research is sometimes the best choice, particularly if you need information written in clear, simple language. To access the information you need to:

- Find the right subject category in the library.
- Search the Contents page and Index of relevant books for your research topic.

11 In pairs, carry out research using the library to find out:
- what waterspouts are
- their link with tornadoes.

12 Now use a search engine to find similar information written in clear and simple language. Which research method is easier?

Key Writing

Wr10 **13 a)** Using ICT, write an opening statement about tornadoes and waterspouts for a young person's information text. Include:
- some of the facts you have researched about tornadoes in Texas
- any facts from the 'Tornado Alley' text that interest you.

Write a rough draft first and then correct it. Then key in the final draft to create a new document.

b) Next, construct a table using the factual information from your research.
- Decide how many columns and rows will be in your table.
- Cut and paste facts and figures from your research document into your table.
- Give your table a heading.

c) Print out your completed page or save it in your own folder.

② Bee attack

Aims

- Read a report about an attack by bees
- Record events and facts in chronological order (S6)
- Create vivid images (W11)
- Write a report

The following account, from *Tea Pests* by J.W. Beagle-Atkins, tells the amazing story of an attack by a swarm of bees. These are highly fierce tree bees related to hornets and any attack would be serious. The events are told by the victim who is out riding at the time.

Buzzing Death

Souvenir jumped, bucked, reared and lashed out in all directions to rid himself of the bees, while I, attempting to protect my face and limbs, had the greatest
5   difficulty in retaining my saddle. In a few moments, an angry buck while turning a corner at full gallop threw me into the dust.

With less than a mile to safety, I began to leg it with far greater determination than I had ever done in my life. But I
10 was covered from head to foot with bees; they crawled in thousands all over me, stinging with excruciating pain. The under-rim of my topee became an angry hive, bees clustered inches deep. My forehead, ears and neck were blanketed in a buzzing, stinging swab of agony. Bees crawled inside my open-
15 necked shirt and up my unprotecting shorts; they were everywhere. I tore them away in handfuls, but only to make room for others about me in clouds.

As I staggered on I yelled frantically to distant workers; but seeing the swarms about me, they bolted in every direction but mine. Gasping for breath, each time I opened my swollen mouth, more bees entered, until my tongue was stung to twice its normal size, and I was crunching them with my teeth. My nostrils had swollen into uselessness; my eyes, stung and running with water, were rapidly closing…

…My timely rescue was effected by two quick-witted Gurkhas, who had raced to a thatch stack and, bringing bundles of dry grass, had quickly surrounded me with a dense wall of fire and smoke, until the bees were beaten off. Later, as I lay unconscious, while the district was being scoured for a doctor, these same two staunch men insisted upon remaining and extracting stings from my inflamed carcass. It took two days to free my body of the discarded stings. When, eventually, I recovered consciousness I was beamingly informed that I had had at least two thousand punctures, probably a record.

I lay in torment for several days, unable to move. My body, blown up like an oversized sausage, was black, blue and purple, and as hard as frozen meat. For several days I could see and speak only with the greatest difficulty, and it took many applications of anti-swelling lotions before what had once been my nose and ears again emerged from the general mess.

My convalescence was a lengthy business of some six months in the hospital and several weeks in the cool hills of Darjeeling.

buck a vertical jump made by a horse
excruciating very painful
topee type of hat or helmet
Gurkhas people from Nepal known for being good soldiers
carcass the dead body of an animal
convalescence the gradual recovery of health after an illness
Darjeeling a hill town in West Bengal

Key Reading

> **Recount texts**
>
> This text is a **recount** or **chronological report**. Its **purpose** is to recount or tell the reader about a series of events in the order in which they happened.
>
> The main features of this text are:
> - It is told in the **past tense**, for example, 'I *yelled* frantically…'
> - It describes events in **time order** (chronological order), for example, we are told that the writer's recovery after the attack 'was a lengthy business of *some six months*…'
> - It uses **time connectives**, for example, '*Later*, as I lay unconscious…'

1 a) Over what period did the events described in the text happen – for example, a week, a month, several months?

b) What happens to the writer by the end of the text?

2 What tense is the text written in?

3 a) Is the text written in the first person or the third person?

b) An autobiography is the story of someone's life written by that person. Is the text an autobiography? Give reasons for your answer.

Purpose

4 a) What is the main purpose of this text? Did the author write it:
- because he survived the attack
- to entertain the reader with a gripping event
- to warn the reader about the dangers of bees
- to thank the Gurkhas for their help?

Point to evidence in the text to support your answer.

b) Which of the other options also fit this text? Give reasons for your answer.

Reading for meaning

Chronological order

Various events happen in the recount *Buzzing Death* and many details are given. This can make it difficult to pick out the main events. However, the text is written in **chronological order**, like a story/narrative. This means we can **sum up the events** in each paragraph on a timeline. For example, the first event in the recount – the attack by a swarm of bees – has been added to the timeline below.

The writer is attacked by a swarm of bees.

Later in paragraph 1, the author recounts how the pony, Souvenir, began to panic. Then the author describes how, 'In a few moments, an angry buck while turning a corner at full gallop threw me into the dust.' So the next main event is: 'His pony threw him into the dust.'

5 Summarise the main events of *Buzzing Death* and add them to your own version of the timeline above. Follow these steps for each paragraph:
- Read the paragraph again.
- Picture in your mind what is happening.
- Sum this up in a single sentence.
- Record this sentence on the timeline.

6 When your timeline is finished, bracket those events that happened *during the attack* and those that happened *after the attack*, as in the example below:

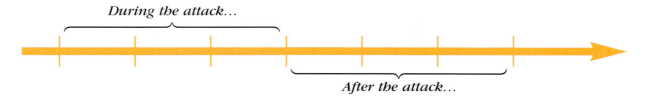

Exploring further: Finding facts

In this recount the writer also includes specific facts, such as names and numbers. To find this information you must read the report differently. You need to **scan** the text for the *exact* information.

7 a) Read through the text quickly and spot the following:
- three names
- a number
- three examples of a period of time, for example, a week.

b) Add these facts to your timeline in the correct place (if they are not already there).

Focus on: Creating images

The writer brings his recount to life with vivid word pictures or **images**. When the bees are attacking in paragraphs 1, 2 and 3, he does this using powerful verbs. In line 1 he could have said:

> Souvenir *jumped* in all directions…

Instead he says:

> Souvenir *jumped, bucked, reared* and *lashed out* in all directions…

These verbs tell the reader just how awful the experience was and give a strong impression of the pony's actions. They also tell the reader how the writer felt.

8 Below are further verbs from the text:
- blanketed
- crawled
- tore
- staggered
- yelled
- bolted.

a) Use a thesaurus to find **synonyms** (words that have similar meanings to these words).

b) Record them in a list and keep them for later – you will use them in question 10.

Exploring further: Adding detail around the verb

The writer sometimes adds phrases around the powerful verbs he uses. For example, the pony is described as having 'jumped, bucked, reared and lashed out'. *Where* did the pony do this? Answer: *'in all directions…'* The phrase 'in all directions' gives further detail and emphasises the drama of the attack.

9 Find similar phrases in these lines. Ask 'where' in each case:
- lines 7–8
- line 12
- lines 16–17.

Key Writing

R3 **10 a)** Imagine that you are attacked by a plague of biting insects, such as mosquitoes. Draw up a table with the following column headings and make short notes under each one. The first column has been started for you, as an example.

Before the attack	During the attack	After the attack
A cloud of mosquitoes approach		
No time to take cover		

b) Use your notes to write a recount of three paragraphs about the attack. Each paragraph should be about 50 words long.

- Use the first person 'I' and the past tense.
- Include specific names and times.
- Use powerful verbs (choose the best from the list you created for question 8).
- Add a phrase around some of your verbs.

Bee attack

3 The Birds

Aims

- Read an extract from a short story, *The Birds*
- Learn ways of extending sentences
- Study the different styles used in the text (S10)
- Discuss in groups, predicting what might happen (S&L11)

The following extract is from the short story *The Birds* by Daphne du Maurier. Nat, a farm worker, and his family live in a small cottage. Autumn has suddenly turned into a bitterly cold winter and during the night some birds have entered the children's bedroom. Earlier they attacked Nat at the window.

'What is it, Nat, what's happened?' his wife called from the further bedroom, and swiftly he pushed the children through the door to the passage and shut it upon them, so that he was alone now, in their bedroom, with the birds.

    He seized a blanket from the nearest bed, and using it as a weapon flung it to right and left about him in the air. He felt the thud of bodies, heard the fluttering of wings, but they were not yet defeated, for again and again they returned to the assault, jabbing his hands, his head, the little stabbing beaks sharp as a pointed fork. The blanket became a weapon of defence; he wound it about his head, and then in greater darkness beat at the birds with his bare hands. He dared not stumble to the door and open it, lest in doing so the birds should follow him.

How long he fought with them in the darkness he could not tell, but at least the beating of the wings about him lessened and then withdrew, and through the density of the blanket he was aware of light. He waited, listened; there was no sound except the fretful crying of the children from the bedroom beyond. The fluttering, the whirring of the wings had ceased.

He took the blanket from him and stared about him. The cold grey morning light exposed the room. Dawn, and the open window, had called the living birds; the dead lay on the floor. Nat gazed at the little corpses, shocked and horrified. They were all small birds, none of any size; there must have been fifty of them lying there upon the floor. There were robins, finches, sparrows, blue tits, larks and bramblings, birds that by nature's law kept to their own flock and their own territory, and now, joining one with another in their urge for battle, had destroyed themselves against the bedroom walls, or in the strife had been destroyed by him. Some had lost feathers in the fight, others had blood, his blood, upon their beaks…

Later that day Nat returns home from the farm to find that there has been a government announcement over the radio. His wife Jill has written it down.

'Statement from the Home Office at eleven a.m. today. Reports from all over the country are coming in hourly about the vast quantity of birds flocking above towns, villages and outlying districts, causing obstructions and damage and even attacking individuals. It is thought that the Arctic air stream, at present covering the British Isles, is causing birds to migrate south in immense numbers, and that intense hunger may drive these birds to attack human beings. Householders are warned to see to their windows, doors and chimneys, and to take reasonable precautions for the safety of their children. A further statement will be issued later.'

lest in case (used to stop something happening)
bramblings finches
Arctic air stream air current coming from the North Pole

Key Reading

Narrative texts

This text is an extract from a **narrative**. Its **purpose** is to tell a story in an entertaining way.

The main features of this text are:

- It has a structure that includes an opening (**introduction**), a problem (**complication**), a dramatic moment or event when everything comes to a head (**crisis**) and an ending (**resolution**) when things are sorted out for good or bad. For example, this extract comes from the middle of the story. A complication has arisen (the birds begin to attack) and the story is building to the crisis.

- It has **characters**, who the story is about. We often hear their words and thoughts.

- It has a **narrator**, who tells the story in either the first person (I/we) or the third person (he/she/it), for example, '…swiftly *he* pushed the children through the door…'

- It features **powerful words**. The language of the narrative must be interesting to read or listen to, for example, 'He felt the *thud* of bodies, heard the *fluttering* of wings…'

1 a) How does the text open? Check the first sentence.
  b) What tense is used in this sentence?

2 Is the story told in the first or the third person?

3 Which kinds of word make this line powerful?
 'Nat gazed at the little corpses, shocked and horrified.'

4 What important information is the reader given at the end of the extract?

Purpose

The purpose of a narrative is to entertain the reader. One way to do this is by catching and keeping the reader's interest. For example, the extract opens with the question: 'What is it, Nat, what's happened?'. This shows that at least one of the characters is unaware of what's going on, and this makes the reader want to know more.

5 What action follows straight after this comment?

6 At what point in paragraph 1 does the reader find out what the problem is? What is the effect of placing the problem here?

Reading for meaning

The Birds is a short story full of description. Many sentences are long and packed with detail. For example, when Nat is in the room with the birds we are told:

> He felt the thud of bodies, heard the fluttering of wings, but they were not yet defeated, for again and again they returned to the assault, jabbing his hands, his head, the little stabbing beaks sharp as a pointed fork.

When reading this long sentence, vivid pictures come tumbling one after the other. If this long sentence was split up into smaller sentences, some of the pace and excitement would be lost. The series of actions that make up the fight would be broken. For example:

> Pauses mean that the sentence loses pace

He felt the thud of bodies, heard the fluttering of wings. *But* they were not yet defeated. *Again* and again they returned to the assault. *They* jabbed his hands, his head, the little stabbing beaks sharp as a pointed fork.

7 Try turning the following two short sentences into one long sentence. Your will need to use a connective such as 'but', 'so' or 'and', and alter the punctuation to match.

> The birds kept pecking at his arms and his head. Time and again he fought them off with the blanket.

Extending sentences

One way in which the writer extends sentences is by using the '-ing' form of the verb. For example, '…they returned to the assault, *jabbing* his hands, his head…'

You can do this by changing different verbs in your own writing. For example, 'It plunged down. It struck the floor with a clatter' could become '*Plunging* down, it struck the floor with a clatter' or 'It plunged down, *striking* the floor with a clatter'.

8 a) Write a paragraph about a bird (or another wild creature) trapped in a room. Include '-ing' verbs at the beginning and in the middle of sentences. Use a thesaurus to find interesting verbs. Start by looking up the following:

- dive
- crawl
- bewilder
- collide
- crush.

b) Try to make the action flow by using longer sentences like the example discussed on page 92.

Exploring further: The semicolon

The semicolon (;) can be used to emphasise two pieces of information about the same thing. It can also lengthen a sentence when it is used instead of a full stop. For example, 'The blanket became a weapon of defence; he wound it about his head…'

9 Find an example of how the semicolon is used in paragraph 4 of the extract. Say what information the semicolon emphasises.

Focus on: Change of style

The final paragraph of the extract is a bulletin from the government warning the country about the attacking birds. It is written in a direct, formal style with few images. This is quite different from the style of the earlier paragraphs. For example, the use of the **passive tense** stresses the formal tone: 'It is *thought* that the Arctic air stream…' (The active tense would be less formal: 'We *think* that the Arctic air stream…')

There are also other features that emphasise the direct, formal style of the bulletin.

10 a) What tense is the bulletin written in?

b) How does this contrast with the tense used in the earlier paragraphs?

11 Find two examples of technical terms used in the bulletin. Explain their meanings.

12 What kind of text would you say the bulletin is *mainly*:
- a recount
- an information text
- an explanation
- a narrative?

Key Speaking and Listening

13 A second bulletin is broadcast from the government later in the story. It begins: 'This is London...'

Working in small groups, discuss what you think the bulletin will say. Consider the following questions:
- Will the government have control of the situation?
- Will the bird attacks have got worse?
- Will the situation be out of control?
- What will happen to Nat? Will he save the day?

Share ideas in your group, listening to and then building on what each person says. One person in your group should make notes of your ideas. Report your ideas to another group and see how they compare.

④ Unit 4 Assignment: The weather forecaster

Assessment Focus

❱ AF2 Produce texts which are appropriate to task, reader and purpose

---

> **You:** are a US weather forecaster.
>
> **Your task:** to write an information leaflet about tornadoes in the USA. The leaflet should include safety advice.

Stage 1

First plan the layout of your leaflet.

- What kind of heading will it have?
- Where will you position subheadings?
- What other layout features will you include?

(You should draw on the work you did on tornadoes earlier in the unit.)

Start with an opening paragraph giving general information on the nature of tornadoes and detailed examples.

Include a second linking paragraph on the damage done by tornadoes.

Use the notes on the next page and any other information you collected on tornadoes earlier in the unit.

Tornadoes:
- travel from the Gulf of Mexico
- paths and danger zones (for example, Tornado Alley)
- speed
- time of year they occur
- tornado may change direction
- TOTO.

Damage:
- coastal damage
- flooding
- damage inland
- power lines down
- severe damage to buildings, roads, crops
- deaths.

Stage 2

Next, include a section giving information on the importance of having access to a storm cellar. Give this section a clear subheading.

Use the following notes to help form your main points:

Important features of a storm cellar:
- a permanent storm cellar
- a windowless room
- equipped with essentials: drinking water, food, first aid kit, torch, radio
- difference between a 'warning' and a 'watch' (the first means a tornado is on the way, the second a tornado is suspected)
- ensure everyone is present in an emergency (all the family, neighbours, pets).

Stage 3

Now write the leaflet, following your plan. Consider these points:
- Use the present tense for presenting things as they are.
- Use the past tense when describing past events.
- Expand your sentences, starting with a general point and illustrating with specific facts.
- Include terms such as 'especially' or 'above all' to emphasise the importance of the key information.

Challenge

Turn some of the information in each section into advice by using imperative verbs and bullet points instead of a full paragraph.

For example:
  'Storm cellars need to be equipped with food, drink...'

becomes:
- 'Make sure your storm cellar is equipped with...'

The advice tips could be presented in separate panels from the paragraphs of information.

Unit 5 Family Drama

1 Billy and his father

Aims

- Read an extract from a film script
- Explore the features of film scripts
- Develop drama skills and techniques (S&L14)
- Explore character, relationships and issues (S&L16)

This extract is from the film script for *Billy Elliot* by Lee Hall. It is about a boy named Billy from north-east England, whose father who is a miner. Billy wants to be a ballet dancer and has an audition with the Royal Ballet school in London, but his family are very poor.

```
         INT. ELLIOT HOUSE.
         DAD'S BEDROOM - DAY.
         We see DAD looking at
         Mum's jewellery.

   5     CUT TO:
         EXT. PAWNSHOP - NEWCASTLE
         DAD walks towards the pawnshop.
         He opens the door and goes in.

         CUT TO:
  10     EXT. STREET - DAY
         DAD and BILLY walk down the road. Dad carries a
         suitcase. Billy dances.
            DAD     Is that absolutely necessary?
                    Walk normal, will you.

  15     CUT TO:
         INT. BUS. MOTORWAY - later.
         BILLY and DAD sit on the bus.
```

pawnshop a shop where people are given money in return for their valuables. They have to pay the money back within a certain time to regain their possessions

Billy looks out at the motorway.

20
    BILLY   So what's it like, like?
    DAD   What's what like?
    BILLY   London.
    DAD   I don't know, son.
                I never made it past Durham.
    BILLY   Have you never been, like?
25
    DAD   Why would I want to go to London?
    BILLY   Well, it's the Capital City.
    DAD   Well, there's no mines in London.
    BILLY   Christ, is that all you think about?

CUT TO:

30
EXT. MOTORWAY – AFTERNOON
From outside the bus we see BILLY look out. The bus becomes a blur as it races past us.

CUT TO:

EXT. ROYAL BALLET SCHOOL – DAY
35
DAD and BILLY walk towards the school.

CUT TO:

INT. ENTRANCE TO ROYAL BALLET SCHOOL – DAY
A RECEPTIONIST is sitting at a desk. BILLY and DAD enter.

40
    RECEP   Can I help you?
    DAD   Billy Elliot. We've come for an audition.
    RECEP   Oh, you mean William Elliot.
    DAD   Yeah, William.
    RECEP   Ah yes. Can you go upstairs, please?
45
Dad glances at the stairs.
    DAD   This way?
    RECE   Yes.
    DAD   Thanks.
They climb the stairs.
50

INT. ROYAL BALLET SCHOOL. CHANGING ROOM – DAY
BILLY walks in past some other boys, SIMON and JOHN.
    SIMON   This your first time?
    JOHN   Yeah.
    SIMON   Cor, I've been doing this for two years now.
55
                (to Billy) Hello. Nerve-racking isn't it? Where are you from?
    BILLY   Everington. County Durham.
    SIMON   Durham? Isn't there an amazing cathedral?
60
    BILLY   Dunno. Never been.

Family drama

Key Reading

Film scripts

This text is a **film script** or **screenplay**. Its **purpose** is to provide a written version of a film for those involved in the film, such as the actors, set designers and director.

The main features of this text are:

- The **layout** is set on the page in a particular way. For example, the names of the characters are separated from the speech, there are no speech marks, it includes information about locations. For example, 'Int' means 'interior' (inside) and 'Ext' means 'exterior' (outside).

- It contains **visual information/directions** to actors. For example, camera instructions such as 'CUT TO:' and 'DAD walks towards the pawnshop. He opens the door and goes in.'

- It has **dialogue/speech** which is usually in quite short **(abbreviated) sentences**. For example:

```
SIMON   This your first time?
JOHN    Yeah.
```

1 In the film, Billy, from a poor mining community in north-east England, decides he wants to be a ballet dancer. Why do you think this might make a good story?

2 Exactly where are Billy and his father going?

3 Find an example of an exterior location and an interior location in the first few lines of the script.

4 Find at least one other piece of visual information that describes what a character does.

5 When Simon says, 'This your first time?', it is a shortening of '(Is) this your first time (at this place)?'
Look at Billy's last two words in the scene. Rewrite them as a full sentence.

Purpose

Lee Hall's purpose in writing this film script is to tell a great story. To do this requires **conflict**. The conflict in *Billy Elliot* occurs partly because Billy's father and brother think it isn't 'manly' to be a ballet dancer. Here is a short extract from earlier in the play:

```
BILLY   I don't see what's wrong with it.
DAD     You know perfectly well what's wrong with it.
BILLY   No, I don't.
DAD     Yes, you do.
BILLY   No, I don't.
DAD     Yes, you bloody well do. Who do you think I am?
```

6 In pairs, read aloud the lines in the extract above. Do it in two different ways:

a) Read it with Billy being quiet and a little frightened, and Dad being angry.

b) Read it with both Billy and Dad getting angrier and louder.

7 The scene is set in the kitchen and Billy and his father are sitting down. Imagine that the following take place during the argument:

a) someone bangs his fist on the table

b) someone stands up

c) someone stares at the other person for a long time before speaking.

Decide *who* might make each of these gestures and *at what point* in the argument.

8 Now act out the scene, including the three gestures from question 7. Does adding the gestures change the way in which the scene works?

Exploring further: Space and place

Another way of changing how a scene comes across is to change where people stand in relation to other people in the scene. For example, here are two alternative ways of playing the kitchen scene:

Option 1:    **Option 2:**

9 Try acting the script lines on page 101 using these alternative placings. How is the meaning of the scene changed? Write a paragraph about each way of playing the scene.

Reading for meaning

 We learn quite a lot about Billy and his father from the extract on pages 98–99.

10 Look at the table below.

   a) Find evidence in the script of the things listed in column 1.

   b) Copy the table and complete column 2, following the first example.

What we find out	Evidence
Billy's father does not have much money.	Billy's father takes his wife's jewellery to the pawnshop.
Billy's father still finds it difficult to accept that Billy likes dancing.	
Billy's father doesn't have much experience of travel.	
Billy is very different from the other boys at the audition.	

Script writers often put themselves in the shoes of the cinema audience. In this example from the extract, it is as if we are watching the film:

- Pronoun 'we'
- Present tense verb

```
CUT TO:
EXT. MOTORWAY - AFTERNOON
From outside the bus we see BILLY look out. The bus
becomes a blur as it races past us.
```

- Present tense verb
- Pronoun 'us'

11 Write your own scene direction to go with the short extract on page 93.
- Use the pronoun 'we'.
- Use the present tense.

Imagine the camera is looking through the window into Billy's kitchen, for example, 'From outside the house, *we see…*'

12 You will have noticed that the film script has very simple scene descriptions. For example, 'CHANGING ROOM – DAY.' Note down at least two other simple settings that the script uses.

Focus on: Creating dramatic performances

13 a) On your own, reread the last section of the extract (when Billy arrives at the Royal Ballet).

b) In a group, agree how you think each of the characters in the extract should behave.

c) Complete a chart like the one below so that you have a record of what your group decides. For column 3, think about how the character can be revealed through his or her voice, gestures, body language and clothes, etc.

Character	What he or she is like	How this can be shown
Receptionist	A snob?	Peers over her glasses at Billy and his dad.
Dad		

Key Speaking and Listening

14 a) Perform the script extract, working in the same groups as for question 13. You will need to decide who will read each part and who will read the directions and actions (only one person should be chosen). Use your notes from question 10 to guide your performance.

b) When you have finished your performance, discuss how it went.
- Was the relationship between Billy and his dad made clear?
- Did the other people in the extract have clear, convincing characters?
- How successful did you think your group's performance was overall?
- How did your group's performance compare with that of other groups?

15 Working on your own, write up your thoughts on your group's performance as a short commentary of approximately 75 words. Use these prompts if you wish:

I thought our group performed the scene…

This was because…

In comparison with other groups, our group's performance was…

Exploring further: Researching technical terms

This screenplay uses fairly basic film directions such as 'Cut to:', 'Int.' (interior) and 'Ext.' (exterior).

16 a) Find out what these terms mean:
- dissolve
- zoom
- pan
- close-up.

b) Decide where in the script you could use each of these terms at least once. For example, would 'Close-up' be suitable when the receptionist speaks?

Writing for *The Simpsons*

Aims

- Read about a script writer for a famous TV programme
- Look at how a key idea is developed in a text (R5)
- Explore different ways of organising sentences within paragraphs (S6)

One of the most well-known family TV programmes is *The Simpsons*. But how does it get written and who are the writers? The following article is about the only female writer on the team and how she came to write for the show.

Writing for *The Simpsons*

When *The Simpsons* writers start to argue about storylines, one voice stands out from the rest – the only woman on the team, Carolyn Omine. But Omine admits she's not afraid to shout as loud and as hard as the boys. After three years writing for the award-winning show she's got used to fighting her corner in the testosterone-loaded atmosphere.

She says: "When I come out with a really nasty joke, I sometimes feel like I'm not the most feminine person in the world. I feel like I go back to being a girl when I get into my own office again."

Emmy Award-winning Omine had spent eight years as a writer on comedy shows in the US before she landed the job with *The Simpsons*. And she had always been so desperate to work on the show, that in all her previous contracts she had insisted on a clause that said she would be freed immediately if she was ever offered the chance to work on an episode.

"Everyone always agreed because they thought there was no chance," she laughs.

Her big chance came when she was recommended to one of the show's executive producers by his brother, who she had been working with. "It was staffing season, which is the time of year when you have to get a job if you're a writer otherwise you're unemployed for a year.

"I had an interview with *The Simpsons*, then it was a month until I heard if I'd got it. I hadn't been offered anything else and I thought for the first time I might be unemployed."

Although she is the only woman writer on the show, she admits that's not rare in US TV comedy. "In everything I've worked on I've always been the only woman, or one of two. I don't think it's about prejudice, I just think there are not so many women trying to be comedy writers.

"Only five per cent of the job is sitting writing a script. You sometimes spend 12 hours a day sitting round a table with the guys shouting over them to be heard. I don't think a lot of women would be comfortable doing that. And I think boys are encouraged far more than girls to be funny."

Writing for *The Simpsons* is very much a team effort. Scripts are put together eight months before the show is screened but there's a lot of tinkering after that and changes are made right up to the last minute to ensure each episode is topical. The stories start with ideas brought in by the writers. Unlike other US TV shows, the network and studio are not allowed to dictate plots or themes in a deal that was thrashed out when *The Simpsons* first began.

testosterone a male hormone, which has been linked to aggression
clause section in a contract

Key Reading

> **Recount texts**
>
> This text is mainly a **recount**. Its **purpose** is to tell the reader about events in someone's life – in this case, the life of Carolyn Omine. However, the second half of the text also **explains** how certain things are done.
>
> The main features of this text are:
>
> - It describes someone's past life. This part is written in the **past tense** and told in **time (chronological) order**, for example, 'Her big chance *came when*…'
>
> - It can also describe **continuing situations** using the **present tense**, for example, these parts in the extract are mostly about what Omine does *now*: 'You sometimes *spend* 12 hours a day *sitting* round a table…'
>
> - It includes references to **time** and **time connectives**, for example, 'Omine had spent *eight years* as a writer…', '…the time of year *when* you have to get a job.'

1 a) What is Carolyn Omine's current job?

  b) In what way is she unusual?

2 How long did Omine have to wait after her interview with *The Simpsons* before she was told if she had got the job?

3 Find another example of a time connective in paragraph 2.

4 In paragraph 8, there are many present tense verbs describing how scripts are put together. Find at least three.

Purpose

This text has several purposes because it deals with several things.

5 In the chart below are two reasons why the text was written. Find evidence for these reasons in the extract. Then add the actual quotations from the text to the second column of the chart.

Purpose	Evidence
To tell us about Carolyn Omine's life as a writer	
To tell us how scripts for *The Simpsons* are written	

Reading for meaning

Another purpose the writer of this text might have is to tell us how difficult it is for a woman writing on a comedy show. This idea can be followed through the text: there are four paragraphs where comments are made about Omine being a woman writer for *The Simpsons*.

6 Find the four paragraphs and note down the first and last word of each one. For example:

> **Reference 1:**
> - Paragraph starting: 'When *The Simpsons* writers…'
> - Paragraph ending: '…testosterone-loaded atmosphere.'

7 How does Omine feel about working with so many men? Is she put off by it?

Exploring further: Team planning

8 On your own, come up with a basic idea for a new episode of *The Simpsons*. It can be very simple. For example, 'Bart wants a new bike but Marge decides he has to be good for a day to get it.'

9 a) Work in a group to share your plot ideas. Do this as briefly as possible. Then discuss the ideas in no more than five minutes and agree on a basic storyline.

b) In your groups, spend ten minutes planning a new episode/story for *The Simpsons*.

c) Be ready to present your group's plan briefly to the class.

Focus on: Organising sentences in paragraphs

10 How many sentences does the following paragraph contain?

> Writing for *The Simpsons* is very much a team effort. Scripts are put together eight months before the show is screened but there's a lot of tinkering after that and changes are made right up to the last minute to ensure each episode is topical.

In the above example, the first sentence acts as an **introduction** (giving a general idea) to the second sentence, which provides **further details**.

11 If the first sentence is placed *after* the second sentence, does it make a difference?

Family drama

12 You can't always change sentences around in a paragraph. Look at the example below:

> When *The Simpsons* writers start to argue about storylines, one voice stands out from the rest – the only woman on the team, Carolyn Omine. But Omine admits she's not afraid to shout as loud and as hard as the boys. *After three years writing for the award-winning show she's got used to fighting her corner in the testosterone-loaded atmosphere.*

What 'show'? How do we know?   Who is 'she'? How do we know?

a) In pairs, discuss whether this paragraph would still make sense if you moved the last sentence to the beginning.

b) How does the last sentence refer back to those before it? (Think about the words 'she' and 'award-winning show'.)

Key Writing

13 Now try organising a paragraph for yourself. You can use up to three sentences from the list below to help you.

- Millions of people around the world tune in every week to watch *The Simpsons*.
- *The Simpsons* is an incredibly popular show.
- Some people never miss an episode and have even cancelled weddings to catch a new one!
- People will do anything to watch *The Simpsons*.
- I watched it even though I had an exam the next day.
- They know they're watching one of the great all-time shows on TV.
- However, behaviour like this could lead to long-term relationship problems!

a) Make sure the first sentence of your paragraph introduces a **general** idea.

b) Your second sentence should expand on your first sentence by giving **further details**.

c) Add a third sentence *only* if it follows on from the first two sentences.

d) Write a short commentary of no more than 50 words explaining *how* and *why* your three sentences work well together.

Exploring further

14 Look back at the text *Writing for The Simpsons*. Are there any paragraphs (including those that only have speech) where you could change the order of the sentences and the paragraph would still make sense?

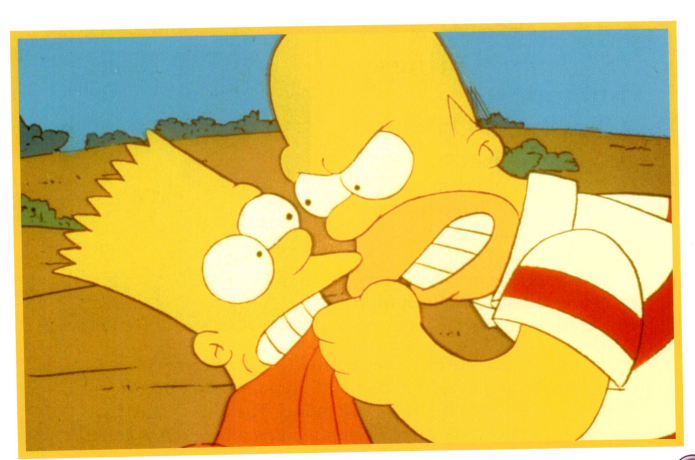

Family drama

3 My Family

Aims

- Read a review of a television programme
- Explore and revise features of reviews
- Write part of your own review (Wr18)
- Distinguish facts from opinions (R6)

My Family **is a situation comedy about an English family. The following text is a preview of the** *My Family* **Christmas 'special'.**

Top TV

My Family brings humour to Christmas Day

My Family, on the BBC, is probably one of my favourite comedy shows of recent years. No matter what the episode, I
5   always end up laughing out loud at the bizarre antics and funny one-liners that issue forth from the Harper family.

And this year's Christmas Day episode is no different. The
10   Harpers, minus Janie, have been out Christmas shopping in London, and are on the Tube, in a tunnel. The train is stuck, for reasons that are never quite clear, providing ample opportunity

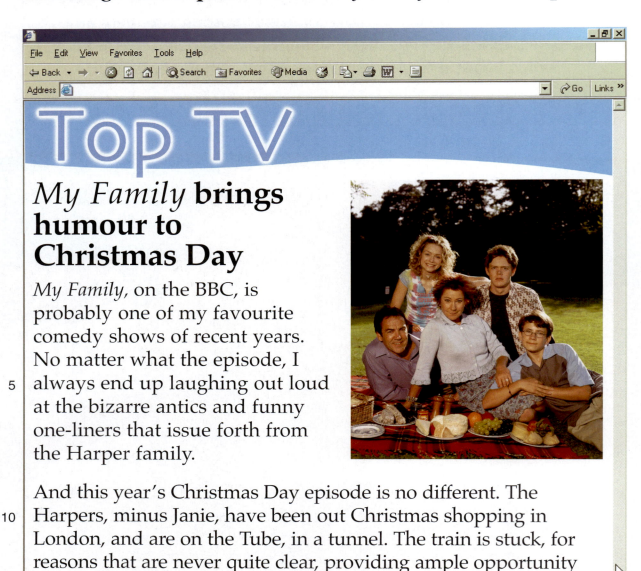

for humour despite the restricted environment. Indeed, the close confines give the actors a chance to really be their characters, with relatively little else to interact with beyond each other. It is as if they've been placed on an empty stage and told to get on with it.

Nick is as stupidly funny as ever, scaring an old woman by suggesting their situation is just like the start of "Cannibal Holocaust". He later sells water to the desperate passengers, all the while denying it to his own father. Ben is as pessimistic as ever, in that hugely funny way that he has. Susan attempts to become the leader of carriage 7, embarrassing herself and her family in the bargain before insulting the driver, who promptly refuses to move the train. Michael goes on several dates with a girl from a few carriages down the train, again showcasing the zaniness of his family by refusing to have anything to do with their world.

As we watch and laugh out loud, we can perhaps give thanks that this isn't our family, and enjoy a well-scripted and acted episode that leaves you hanging on for season five of this wonderful comedy.

pessimistic expects the worst

Key Reading

Review texts

This text is a **review** of a television programme. Its **purpose** is to inform the reader about the programme and give an opinion of how good or bad it is.

The main features of this text are:

- It provides **key information** about the story and characters, for example, 'The Harpers, minus Janie, have been out Christmas shopping in London…' (story); 'Nick is as stupidly funny as ever…' (character).

- It gives the reader an idea of what the reviewer's **opinion** is, through the words and phrases selected, for example, in '…one of my *favourite* comedy shows…', the adjective 'favourite' reveals how much the writer likes it.

- It is written mainly in the **present tense**, even though the reviewer has already seen the programme. For example, 'Michael *goes on* several dates with a girl…'

- It contains **sentences packed with detail**, to give as much information as possible. For example:

    > Susan attempts to become the leader of carriage 7, embarrassing herself and her family in the bargain before insulting the driver, who promptly refuses to move the train.

Note the **three separate sections** of information following the introductory part (the first clause).

1 Does the subtitle of the review provide any clues as to what the reviewer thinks of the programme? Give reasons for your answer.

2 Find other examples of key information in the review. For example:
- What else are we told about the plot in paragraph 2?
- What are we told about Ben in paragraph 3?

3 Identify one other sentence that is packed with detail from paragraph 3.

Purpose

The writer wants the reader to share her enthusiasm for the programme. She does this by:
- mentioning some of the funny moments from the story
- encouraging the reader (through her language) to watch the programme.

4 Look at the last paragraph. The writer says five positive things about the show. Find the exact word or phrase that she says about each of these things:

a) laughter

b) what it makes her think about her own family

c) the acting and writing

d) a phrase meaning 'waiting impatiently'

e) a word meaning 'fantastic' or 'great'.

Reading for meaning

The characters in the programme are described in two ways. On the one hand, the reviewer uses very **simple descriptions**, such as 'Nick is stupidly funny…' and 'Ben is as pessimistic as ever'.

However, when it comes to the reviewer's description of Susan, the reader has to **infer** what sort of person she is from what she does. That is, the reader has to work out what is meant beneath the surface meaning.

5 Read the following information about Susan. Then write down two sentences to describe her.

> Susan attempts to become the leader of carriage 7, embarrassing herself and her family in the bargain before insulting the driver, who promptly refuses to move the train.

Exploring further: Long sentences

The example above contains a lot of detail packed into one long sentence. Why hasn't the writer broken it into three or four shorter sentences? One possible reason is because several shorter sentences wouldn't give the feel of a **series of comic events**.

6 Try breaking the long sentence into four sentences, to see the effect. Begin like this:
'Susan attempts to become the leader of carriage 7. Then, she…'

Focus on: Recognising bias and objectivity

It is natural to expect a review of a TV programme to reflect the reviewer's opinion and be **biased** either for or against it. In fact, it is almost impossible for a reviewer to be **objective** – to make comments or decisions without allowing his or her feelings to get in the way of the facts. This is especially difficult with a television comedy, because what makes each viewer laugh will be very different.

7 What TV programmes make you laugh? Talk with a partner about them and try to identify what it is that you find funny. Say something about:
- the situations and characters
- the storylines.

8 Read the following extracts from two other reviews of *My Family*:

> **Review 1**
> The Christmas episode takes place on a tube train. Ben, Susan, Nick and younger brother Michael are all trapped on it, and they each try to get through it in different ways.

> **Review 2**
> This rather stupid Christmas episode takes place on a tube train – how original! Ben – irritating and unfunny, Susan – even more irritating, and Nick (completely unbelievable) are stuck on a train, along with Michael, the youngest child in the Harper family.

a) Which review is objective – just deals with the facts and what happens?

b) Which review takes a definite point of view?

c) What is the point of view taken by the reviewer? Is it good or bad? How do you know?

Exploring further: Direct address

A more subtle way in which a reviewer gets the reader to agree with his or her opinion is by using **direct address** – addressing the reader as 'us' or 'you'. This makes the reader feel as though he or she is watching the programme with the reviewer.

9 How does the reviewer do this in the last paragraph of the extract?

My Family

Key Writing

Here are some key facts about the film *Billy Elliot*, which was discussed earlier in this unit.

- About a boy from Newcastle who wants to be a ballet dancer.
- Decides to dance rather than box.
- Dad and brother are miners. They are on strike.
- Family doesn't have much money.
- Billy is taught by Mrs Wilkinson.
- Goes to London for an audition.

10 a) Write one paragraph about the film which just mentions the **facts** about the story and characters. You could start like this: 'The film is about…'

b) Now write a second paragraph in which you add some sort of **personal opinion** or comment (good or bad) about the characters or story. For example, you could start:

- 'Billy seems to me…'
- 'I find the story is…'

c) Try to pack some **extra detail** into this second paragraph by lengthening one or two of your sentences with a phrase describing a character or action. For example: 'The fact that the family have little money is made painfully clear by the Dad's trip to the pawnbroker's – *a heart-rending moment.*'

④ Unit 5 Assignment: Drama reviewer

Assessment Focus

▸ AF2 Produce texts which are appropriate to task, reader and purpose

You: write reviews and previews for the local newspaper of plays, musicals, shows (for example, comedians and magicians), gigs and concerts (pop or rock bands, singers) and drama within local schools.

Your task: to write a preview of a piece of drama or a show that you have seen ahead of public screening. Ideally, this should be for a real show or drama, but you can make it up if you wish.

Stage 1

Make notes about the performance. Use a table like the one below to help you. (The first parts have been filled in as an example.)

Name or description of the show or performance.	West Side Story
When and where it is on.	November 15th to 19th, 7.30 pm, Ridgeway High School
Who is in it.	Simon Larwood as Tony; Lia Iqbal as Maria.
What happens. (The main story/facts.)	A boy and girl from opposing gangs in New York fall in love and...
Words that show your opinion of the performance and the people in it. (Pack in as much detail as possible, using *adverb + adjective* phrases.)	
A statement summing up what you thought of it overall.	

Stage 2

Now take the content of your table and plan your paragraphs. Decide what you will put in each of your four paragraphs, starting with an introduction as outlined in the plan below.

> **Paragraph 1:** a general introduction about the performance saying who is putting it on, where and when, and something about how good or bad it is.
>
> **Paragraph 2:**
>
> **Paragraph 3:**
>
> **Final Paragraph:**

Stage 3

Write paragraph 1. Start by making a general comment or statement such as:

> Ridgeway High School's production of *West Side Story*, which can be seen at the school every day this week, is terrifically good…

Use **separate clauses** to add information

Use the **present tense**

Remember to use **adverb + adjective phrases** like this to pack in detail and express your opinion

Then write the remaining three paragraphs.
- Make sure each paragraph is separate.
- Make sure each character or performer is summed up.
- Add what you think by using short words or phrases (for example, 'incredibly powerful') and longer statements (for example, 'You should see this great performance by…')
- Use direct address, involving the reader.

Challenge

Write a review about your own performance in a play, concert or group work in class.
- Write it mostly in the **past tense**.
- Include **basic information** about the performance.
- **Give your opinion**, looking back at what you did objectively and analysing its good and bad points.
- End by summing up your **overall view** of the performance.

Unit 6 Refugees

1 Refugee Boy

Aims

- Read an extract from a narrative text
- Develop the skill of looking for key ideas
- Look at the way an author uses patterns to establish ideas (R5)
- Write your own introduction to a story

The following text is from the opening of a novel called *Refugee Boy* by Benjamin Zephaniah.

Chapter 1
Ethiopia

As the family lay sleeping, soldiers kicked down the door of the house and entered, waving their rifles around erratically and shouting at the top of their voices. Alem ran into the room where his parents were, to find that they had been dragged out of bed dressed only in their nightclothes, and forced to stand facing the wall.

5

The soldier who was in command went and stood so that his mouth was six inches away from Alem's father's ear and shouted, "What kind of man are you?"

Alem's father shuddered with fear; his voice trembled as he replied,

10 "I am an African."

Alem looked on terrified as the soldier shot a number of bullets into the floor around the feet of his father and mother.

His mother screamed with fear. "Please leave us! We only want peace."

The soldier continued shouting. "Are you Ethiopian or Eritrean? Tell

15 us, we want to know."

"I am an African," Alem's father replied.

The soldier raised his rifle and pointed it at Alem's father. "You are a traitor." He turned and pointed the rifle at Alem's mother. "And she is the enemy." Then he turned and pointed the rifle at Alem's forehead. "And he is a mongrel."

Turning back to Alem's father, he dropped his voice and said, "Leave Ethiopia or die."

Chapter 2
Eritrea

As the family lay sleeping, soldiers kicked down the door of the house and entered, waving their rifles around erratically and shouting at the top of their voices. Alem ran into the room where his parents were, to find that they had been dragged out of bed dressed only in their nightclothes, and forced to stand facing the wall.

The soldier who was in command went and stood so that his mouth was six inches away from Alem's mother's ear and shouted, "What kind of woman are you?"

Alem's mother shuddered with fear; her voice trembled as she replied, "I am an African."

Alem looked on terrified as the soldier shot a number of bullets into the floor around the feet of his mother and father.

His father screamed with fear. "Please leave us! We only want peace."

The soldier continued shouting. "Are you Eritrean or Ethiopian? Tell us, we want to know."

"I am an African," Alem's mother replied.

The soldier raised his rifle and pointed it at Alem's mother. "You are a traitor." He turned and pointed the rifle at Alem's father. "And he is the enemy." Then he turned and pointed the rifle at Alem's forehead. "And he is a mongrel."

Turning back to Alem's mother, he dropped his voice and said, "Leave Eritrea or die."

Ethiopia a country in North East Africa, on the Red Sea
Eritrea a country in North East Africa, on the Red Sea. It became part of Ethiopia in 1952 but a war of independence was fought from 1961 until 1993
erratically in an unpredictable way
mongrel an insulting name for someone of mixed parentage; it is usually used to describe animals

Key Reading

Narrative texts

This is a **narrative** text.

The main features of this text are:

- It has a structure that includes an opening (**introduction**), a problem (**complication**), a dramatic moment when everything comes to a head (**crisis**) and an ending (**resolution**) when things are sorted out. Since this is the beginning of a novel, only the introduction and problem are present. However, we can predict the possible crisis and ending from the title of the novel – *Refugee Boy*.
- It has **characters** who the story is about. We often hear their words (in direct speech) and thoughts.
- There is also a **narrator**, who tells the story in either the first person (I/we) or the third person (he/she/it), for example, 'as *he* replied, "I am an African."'
- It uses **powerful words**. The language of the narrative must be interesting to read or listen to, for example, 'Alem's mother *shuddered* with fear.'

1 Where is the problem or complication introduced in each chapter?

2 The story is written by an 'all-knowing' narrator.

   a) Which of the three main characters does it focus on?

   b) How can you tell this?

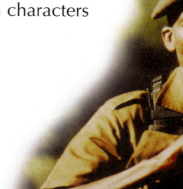

3 a) Find a piece of direct speech in Chapter 1.

  b) Identify two words that show Alem's father's emotions in paragraph 3.

4 The word 'turned' or 'turning' is used three times in the last two paragraphs of both chapters. What does this show about the way the commanding officer is moving?

Purpose

5 a) Below are four purposes of the opening of a novel. Which is the main purpose of this opening?

- to provide a dramatic opening to the story
- to set up the problem or complication
- to introduce the main characters
- to make the reader want to know what happens next.

Point to the evidence in the text to support your choice.

  b) Are any of the other purposes also true of this opening?

Reading for meaning

6 a) Where does Chapter 1 take place? What nationality is Alem's father?

  b) Where does Chapter 2 take place? What nationality is Alem's mother?

7 What must have happened to the family between Chapter 1 and Chapter 2?

8 Briefly summarise the main differences between Chapters 1 and 2, using a table like the one below.

Chapter 1	Chapter 2
Takes place in…	Takes place in…

9 Why do you think the writer has made these two chapters so similar? Write a sentence to explain what effect this has.

. . . .

Focus on: Patterns of language

The writer of this text has selected his words very carefully to make a point about the way human beings behave. One way he has done this is through repetition of ideas and words or phrases.

10 What are the main things that the writer repeats in both chapters?

11 Find more examples of repetition within Chapter 1, where the author uses the same or similar words. Make a list like the one below and try to think of a reason for each use of repetition.

Repeated word or phrase	Reason
rifle	Keeps the idea of a powerful weapon in the reader's mind

A second pattern in this text is the use of words that describe the way people speak.

12 a) In pairs, list all the words that describe the way characters speak. For example, 'shouted' in paragraph 2.

b) Underline the words used for the way the soldiers speak. What differences are there between these words and the words used for the way Alem's mother and father speak?

When a writer establishes a pattern, any break in that pattern is especially noticeable.

13 What is the effect of the soldier lowering his voice at the end of each chapter?

Exploring further: Using quotations

When you write about a text, it is good be able to use quotations effectively as evidence for your views. Here are two basic rules for using quotations:

- make your point first and then use a quotation to support it
- only quote a few words or lines at most.

For example:

> It is clear that the soldier in command speaks aggressively from words like 'shouted', 'his mouth was six inches away' and…

Wr17

14 Write a short paragraph about the differences in the way the speech of the soldiers and the family are described in Chapter 1. Using your list from question 11, include one or two short quotes to support each point.

Key Writing

The extract is told by a **third-person** narrator who is outside the story. This is a good way to tell a complicated story as it means many different points of view can be presented.

Another way of telling the story would have been to use a **first-person** narrator. First-person narrative has a single point of view, usually that of one of the characters.

15 In pairs, discuss whether a first- or third-person narrator is best for a complex story with strong emotions such as Alem's.

16 Rewrite Chapter 1 (lines 1–22) from Alem's point of view, using first-person narrative. You will need to think about:

- what he saw and heard
- how he felt about the treatment of his parents
- how he felt when the rifle was pointed at him
- his worst fear.

Remember to:

- use 'I' for the narrator of the story (Alem)
- include a few extra details about how Alem reacts/feels, using powerful language.

You could start:

'I was sleeping peacefully one night when…'

Refugees and asylum seekers in the UK

Aims

- Read an information text
- Discuss the issues it raises
- Make notes in different forms
- Examine methods of presentation
- Express your own opinions (S&L10, S&L12)

The following extract is from the Commission for Racial Equality's website.

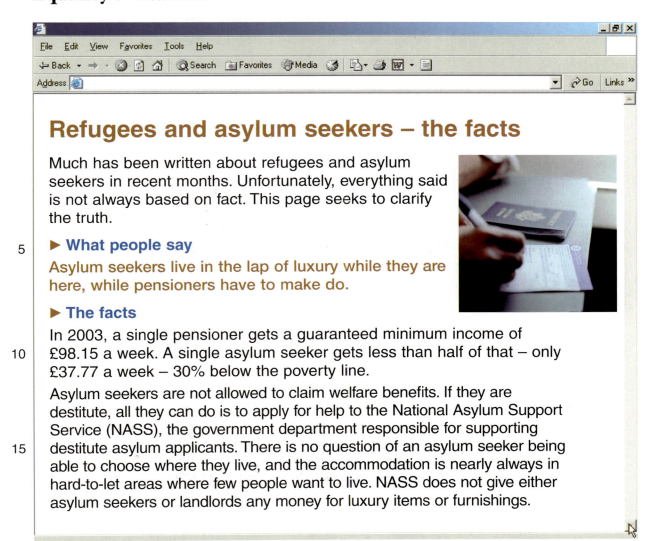

Refugees and asylum seekers – the facts

Much has been written about refugees and asylum seekers in recent months. Unfortunately, everything said is not always based on fact. This page seeks to clarify the truth.

▶ **What people say**

5 Asylum seekers live in the lap of luxury while they are here, while pensioners have to make do.

▶ **The facts**

In 2003, a single pensioner gets a guaranteed minimum income of
10 £98.15 a week. A single asylum seeker gets less than half of that – only £37.77 a week – 30% below the poverty line.

Asylum seekers are not allowed to claim welfare benefits. If they are destitute, all they can do is to apply for help to the National Asylum Support Service (NASS), the government department responsible for supporting
15 destitute asylum applicants. There is no question of an asylum seeker being able to choose where they live, and the accommodation is nearly always in hard-to-let areas where few people want to live. NASS does not give either asylum seekers or landlords any money for luxury items or furnishings.

▶ What people say

Refugees and asylum seekers increase unemployment and take jobs away from the host population.

▶ The facts

There is no evidence that refugees and asylum seekers take jobs away from the host population.

Asylum seekers are not permitted to work despite evidence that they would prefer to support themselves than rely on the State. On getting status refugees pay taxes and generally contribute as others do. Higher proportions of foreign-born workers, including refugees, work in construction, cleaning, agriculture and manufacturing than native workers, reflecting the contribution they make to the less popular industries. There is also reliance on migrants to fill the gaps present in the UK labour market: according to the Greater London Authority, 23% of doctors and 47% of nurses working within the NHS were born outside the UK.

The UK's working population is declining. The UN's Population Division reports that low birth rates mean the EU will need to import 1.6 million migrants a year simply to keep its working-age population stable between now and 2050.

▶ What people say

Asylum seekers are just a huge expense to the British taxpayer.

▶ The facts

A recent Home Office study found that, far from being a burden on UK taxpayers, migrants made a net contribution of approximately £2.5 billion to income tax in 1999–2000. Throughout history, migrants (including refugees) have made invaluable contributions to our economic and cultural life, for example:

- ▶ fish and chips were brought to the UK by 17th-century Jews expelled from Portugal;
- ▶ Alec Issigonis, who fled the war between Turkey and Greece, was the brain behind the Mini and the Morris Minor;
- ▶ Karl Marx and Sigmund Freud were refugees; and
- ▶ Sir John Hoblon, the first Governor of the Bank of England, was the grandson of an asylum seeker from France.

---

asylum seeker a person asking to be allowed to stay in another country

refugee a person who has been forced to leave their country because it is not safe for them to stay

poverty line people who live below the poverty line suffer hardship through lack of money

destitute completely without money

host population the people of the country where asylum is applied for

status officially recognised as refugees

proportions part of the total number

migrants people moving from one country to another

labour market total of jobs to be filled

net contribution added overall

Key Reading

> **Information texts**
>
> This text is an **information** text. Its **purpose** is to give clear information about a topic.
>
> The main features of this text are:
> - It consists of a **introductory statement** followed by **logically ordered sections**. For example, Introduction – 'Much has been written about refugees and asylum seekers in recent months'.
> - Verbs are in the **present tense**, for example, 'Asylum seekers *are* not allowed to claim welfare benefits'
> - It uses **headings** and **subheadings** to make it easier to find information, for example, 'What people say'.
> - Both **general information** and **specific facts**, often using **technical language**, are included, for example, 'Karl Marx and Sigmund Freud were refugees' and 'migrants made a *net contribution* of approximately £2.5 billion'.

1 After the introduction, each of the three sections is organised in the same way. Describe how each section is organised.

2 Most of the text is in the present tense. Which section is in the past tense, and why?

3 a) Explain each of these technical terms:
- guaranteed minimum income
- construction industry
- native population

b) What is the effect of using technical terms in this information text?

4 The text uses several **acronyms** – a series of letters where each letter stands for a word. It explains only one of these: NASS.

a) Find three examples of acronyms in the text.

b) Find out what the letters stand for in each case?

Purpose

5 a) In pairs, discuss whether you think the main purpose of this text is:
- To inform people about asylum seekers.
- To correct some people's ideas about asylum seekers.
- To start a debate about asylum seekers.
- To give some historical facts about asylum seekers.

b) Are any of the other purposes also true of this web page?

6 Why do you think the Commission for Racial Equality (CRE) decided that a web page giving this information was necessary?

Reading for meaning

7 a) The web page is packed with facts. Look again at each of the three main sections and write down the comment each section begins with, in a table like the one below.

b) Then find at least three specific facts in each section that give information on the comment. Add these in note form in your table.

Comment 1: *Asylum seekers live in… luxury… here, while pensioners have to make do.*	Comment 2:	Comment 3:
Single pensioner gets £98.15 a week; asylum seeker gets £37.77.		

c) Be ready to share your findings with the class.

R8

8 Another way of presenting this information, as a kind of plan, is to make it into a spidergram. Try to 'translate' the notes in your table into a spidergram like the one begun below.

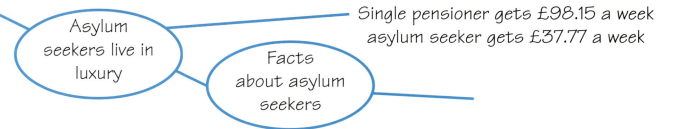

9 Look at the bullet points in section 3 of the text. What two things do the people listed here have in common?

- -

Focus on: Organising information on a webpage

Scrolling versus turning

In a long paper-based text you get to the next piece of information by turning the page. In a long computer-based text you get to the next piece of information by scrolling down the screen using the mouse or an arrow key.

10 a) How do paper-based texts help the reader to navigate around the whole text? Think of three features.

   b) How does the reader get to the information they need quickly?

11 a) How do computer-based texts help the reader to navigate around the whole site or document? Think of two features. Refer back to the website on pages 129–130, if necessary.

   b) How does the reader get to the information they need quickly?

Design layout

The CRE text is from a web page and is designed to give people information quickly and easily.

12 In pairs, discuss the design features of the page that make it easy for readers to find information. You might consider:
- repeated features
- font size
- use of bold type
- bullet points
- use of numbers or percentages.

13 With your partner, decide which of the above design features could be used to present or highlight this type of information more clearly.

Key Speaking and Listening

 14 The CRE information is designed as a webpage. You are going to use the same information to produce a formal presentation for your class on how refugees live in the UK and what they have achieved.

a) In pairs, work through the information in your tables from question 7. Select which pieces of information from each of the three sections you will include in your five minute presentation.

b) Next, decide who will present each of the sections, or whether you will share the presentation of each section, for example with one person speaking and the other displaying charts or figures.

c) Plan your visual aids, for example, prepare a bar chart of information about incomes, write key figures for display on an OHT or summarise a series of examples on a powerpoint screen. Write key points on prompt cards to remind you what to say next.

d) Rehearse your presentation to ensure the links between sections are smooth. Try to vary your pace so that the information remains clear and interesting for your audience. Be ready to make your presentation.

Remember to:
- use the present tense mostly, but the past tense when referring to past events
- move from each general point to a specific example
- include necessary technical terms but always explain them the first time they are used
- make each point as clearly as you can. Avoid long rambling sentences.

3 Student action

Aims

◗ Read an advice text
◗ Think about audiences for texts
◗ Look at how advice texts are organised
◗ Explore different degrees of formality in written texts
◗ Practise writing an advice text (Wr15)

The following text is from a leaflet aimed at students who are concerned about the treatment of asylum seekers in the UK.

STAR
(Student Action for Refugees)

**Refugee Policy is PANTS campaign
Campaign Action 5: Section 55
Write to/Visit your local MP**

Students are especially well placed to lobby those in positions of influence because you are new voters with whom politicians want to engage and you have a strong collective voice. Writing a letter to or meeting your MP is a simple and effective way of campaigning; it is your chance to inform your MP of the issues and it adds to the voice for refugees.

It is your right as a voter to let your local MP know about issues of concern to you and your local community. It is also part of your MP's job to read and reply to letters from constituents.

Having been involved in STAR and having volunteered with local refugee agencies/projects **you are likely to be more informed about refugee and asylum issues than your local MP**. MPs are expected to answer questions from constituents on a diverse range of subjects, so won't have in-depth knowledge of many issues. You will be able to give them the facts and tell them the reality from your experiences!

You can also ask your MP to raise your concerns with the Home Secretary, who is obliged to respond. If a significant number of MPs ask questions on a particular issue then the Home Secretary is forced to take action.

To find out who your local MP is, call the House of Commons Information Office 020 7219 4272.

You might also be able to get hold of your MP, at their constituency office. You should be able to find out the phone number at a local library or town hall or by searching under their name on the Internet.

Visit your MP…

At Westminster – You can arrange to visit your MP in the Central Lobby in parliament, when the House of Commons is sitting. You will need to make an appointment to see them, to check they're going to be around. NB You need special permission to organise a mass lobby.

In their constituency – MPs also hold regular 'surgeries' in their constituencies (find out the details from their office), and groups such as STAR often visit their local MPs. Take along three/four people and decide who will speak about which issue. Be clear about what you would like to get from the meeting: request a parliamentary question on Section 55 or the MP's support for STAR's campaign. Ask them for their personal opinion about the issue and be polite and concise in stating your concerns.

Invite your MP to visit campus

Why not go one step further and ask for your MP to be a speaker at one of your STAR meetings. Use the Campaign Action on Section 55 as a reason to invite them and take the opportunity to advertise the meeting well to get lots of students along to ask questions. You could also arrange a photo opportunity as an added incentive for your MP to attend, and get some coverage in the student press.

- Don't forget to give them a STAR leaflet and the Campaign briefing.

Section 55 a government ruling which takes away National Asylum Support Service support from asylum applicants who do not apply for asylum as soon as they reach the UK
pants (slang) very bad
campus the site of a university
lobby try and influence a member of parliament
positions of influence having political power
issues of concern things that are worrying
constituents the people who live in the area that elects an MP
obliged have no choice
surgeries times when an MP is available for meetings with his or her constituents
photo opportunity a chance for newspapers to take a photograph

Key Reading

> ### Advice texts
>
> This is an **advice** text. Its **purpose** is to advise the reader to do (or not to do) something.
>
> The main features of this text are:
>
> - It has a **series of points** in a **logical order**, for example, 'Invite your MP to visit campus'.
> - It uses **direct address**, using **imperatives** or the words 'you' or 'your'. For example, '*Be* clear about what *you* would like to get from the meeting'
> - It uses **formal language** but an **informal tone** where suited to the audience. For example, 'Refugee Policy is PANTS'.
> - It has a **design layout** which helps to make the structure of the advice clear. For example, subheadings to show sections of advice.

1 The campaigners decided to use the slang term 'pants' as the title of their campaign. How would this appeal to their student audience?

2 Look closely at the use of direct address in section 1, 'Write to/Visit your local MP'. What effect does the constant use of 'you' and 'your' have on the reader?

3 a) What three pieces of advice are given in paragraph 2, section 2, 'Visit your MP'?

   b) Find the three imperative verbs that signal this.

   c) Can you find any phrases that 'soften' the imperative in section 2, like this example: '*You will need* to make an appointment…'

4 What is the purpose of the bullet point right at the end of the leaflet?

Grammar for reading

Imperative verbs **tell** (or **command**) you directly to do something. For example: '*Write* to your MP as soon as you can'.

In advice texts, imperatives are often 'softened' by adding phrases like '*Try to* write to your MP as soon as you can'.

Purpose

The **purpose** of this advice text is to help students in higher education campaign on the issue of refugees.

 5 a) In pairs, discuss how the organisation of the text makes the advice clear and interesting. Think about its use of:

- headings and subheadings
- bold text.

b) Make a list of the subheadings and summarise in one sentence the main point of advice being given in each, for example:

> Write to/Visit your local MP: main point – Writing a letter to or meeting your MP is a simple and effective way of campaigning.

6 The leaflet indicates that students reading it will have had some experience of organising a campaign before. Find a sentence in section 2 that tells you this.

Reading for meaning

Advice texts not only give clear pieces of advice, they also back them up with good **reasons** for taking the advice. For example, in section 1 a number of reasons are put forward for why writing to an MP will be effective.

> 1. Students are new voters so MPs will listen to them.
> 2. As constituents, they have the right to talk to their MP.
> 3.

7 What is the third reason given to support this piece of advice?

The main points in an advice text can also be backed up by **examples** or by **expanding** the main point. This technique is used later in the leaflet. For example, in section 2, under the subheading 'At Westminster' the main point is expanded like this:

1. Be sure to make an appointment to see your MP.
2. Seek special permission for a mass lobby.

8 Look again at the last two pieces of advice under the subheadings 'In their constituency' and 'Invite your MP to visit campus'. Note down the two points that expand each piece of advice. Refer back to your list of advice from question 5b, if it helps.

Focus on: Formal language, informal tone

The advice in this text is on a serious matter and introduces some complicated ideas. The writer has therefore chosen **formal language** to match his topic. For example, this sentence uses formal language to put across an idea about the way a political process works:

> If a significant number of MPs ask questions on a particular issue, then the Home Secretary is forced to take action.

It uses a **conditional sentence** structure to do this.

9 Read the following pairs of sentences. Then rewrite them as one longer conditional sentence using 'if' and 'then'.
- Arrange a photo opportunity on campus.
- It is much more likely that your MP will attend.
- Seek special permission from your MP.
- You will be able to hold a mass lobby.

Grammar for reading

Conditional sentences usually have two parts or clauses. In the first a condition is set by the connective *if*; in the second the result of completing the condition is stated, often using the connective *then*.

Contracted words or phrases show where a letter has been missed out by an apostrophe. For example: *don't* instead of *do not*. In writing they create an informal effect.

Exploring further: Impersonal language

The STAR text also includes impersonal language – another feature of formal writing. Examples of this are sentences or clauses that start with the words 'It is…' For example, in section 1, 'it is your chance to inform your MP' sounds more distanced than 'which is…' or 'this is…'.

10 a) Find two more examples of 'It is…' sentences in section 1.

   b) Try rewriting them to sound more personal and less distant.

However, the writer of this advice also keeps his audience of students aged 18–22 in mind. He uses some features of informal language to keep them interested.

11 In pairs, look through the text to find examples of the following features:
- informal words or phrases
- direct address
- contracted words or phrases
- punctuation for humorous effect.

Be ready to share your findings.

Key Writing

Wr15 **12** The STAR campaign manager has asked you to produce a poster based on the advice in the leaflet. The aim is to pass on the key points to students and encourage them to contact their MPs.

a) Reread your list of main points and reasons or expanded points from questions 5, 7 and 8. Then choose the four points you will use for the poster. Arrange them in the most effective order.

b) Find or draw one image that will help give your advice impact.

c) Decide on a heading for your poster, using the campaign name.

d) Write out your four points. Remember to:
- use imperatives to tell the reader the main point
- use some informal language to appeal to the reader
- highlight key words using bold or underlining.

Exploring further

Try using IT resources to give your poster idea more impact.

- Scan in your image.
- Choose a distinct font for your heading.
- Experiment with different fonts and colours to make each piece of advice clear.

④ Unit 6 Assignment: How to write to an MP

Assessment Focus

❱ AF2 Produce texts which are appropriate to task, reader and purpose

> **You:** are a campaign organiser.
>
> **Your task:** to design a leaflet advising students how to write a letter to their MP.

Stage 1

Begin by planning the different sections of your leaflet. Here are some section headings. Select the four most important headings for your purpose.

- Advice on how to find out who your MP is and how to contact him/her (take this from the STAR leaflet)
- Advice on formal letter layout
- Advice on getting involved with other STAR campaigns
- Advice on the content of the letter
- Encouragement to write the letter as soon as possible
- Details of the next STAR meeting.

Decide in which order to place your four sections.

Stage 2

Draft your first section – try to give general advice on the purpose of the leaflet and how to get in touch with the MP.

Next, introduce how to lay out a formal letter. Decide how you will present the diagram below in your leaflet.

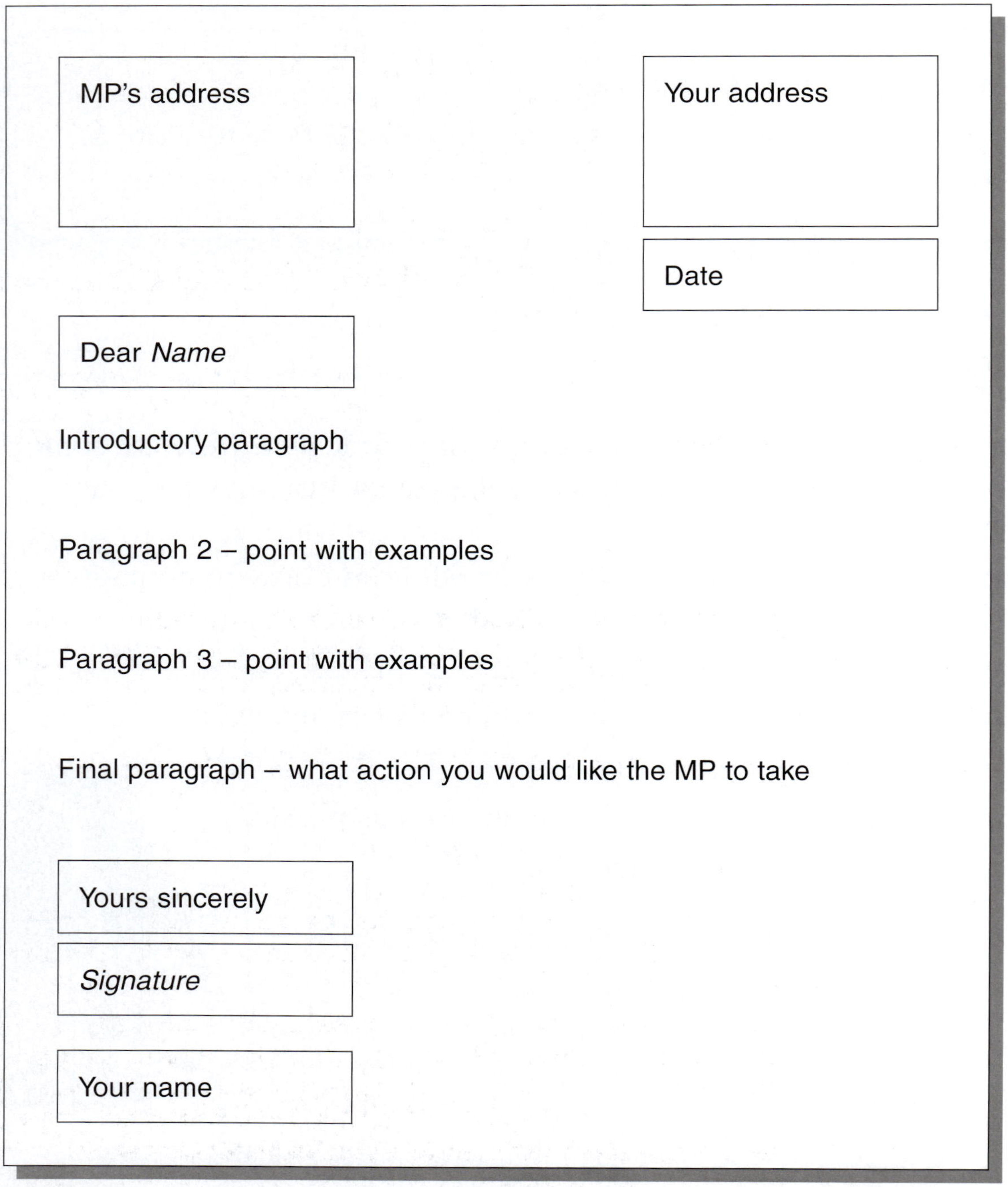

MP's address		Your address
		Date

Dear *Name*

Introductory paragraph

Paragraph 2 – point with examples

Paragraph 3 – point with examples

Final paragraph – what action you would like the MP to take

Yours sincerely

Signature

Your name

Will you add notes around the edge to show the purpose of each feature? Will you include a paragraph or bullet points above the diagram?

Think about how you will present advice on the content of the four paragraphs in the letter. Here are points you need to include:

- the introduction and what should be said in it
- suggestions about the points to make in the second and third paragraphs
- suggestions for the examples in paragraphs 2 and 3 – you can use the information in texts 1 and 2 for ideas about this
- advice about how to conclude the letter.

Finally, decide how you will round off the leaflet. What are the key points you will remind students about? Complete your first draft.

Stage 3

Look back over your draft to see if you can improve it.

Remember to:

- use imperative verbs for the main advice points
- include a reason or expand on each piece of advice
- use direct address
- use some formal language to emphasise important ideas, e.g. 'It is', 'There are'
- make the tone informal in places to keep the reader's interest, for example, contracted words, informal words/phrases.

Challenge

Experiment with some of the imperatives you use by adding phrases, such as 'Try to…' and 'Why not…', to soften the effect of the command.

Unit 7 New media

1 The Birth of The Bug

Aims

- Read an advert for a digital radio and explore how it adapts its language to suit a particular audience and purpose (S9)
- Analyse the underlying meaning of a cartoon strip
- Think about how texts are shaped by the technology they use (R9)
- Give a presentation in a persuasive way (S&L4)

The following text is an advert in a gadget magazine.

The Birth of The Bug

The Bug is one seriously cool collaboration between yours truly, Wayne Hemingway of hEMINGWAYdESIGN (the founders of award winning label Red or Dead and acclaimed designers of all things affordable from wallpapers through to housing estates), and PURE Digital (pioneers of DAB digital radio, and the guys behind the best-selling trannie in the UK – the PURE EVOKE-1).

The Bug may look cool on your coffee table but it also performs – men in white coats have stroked their pointy beards over this till their chins became sore – and gives radio clarity and a choice of stations that will make you want to take your existing FM/AM units down to your local Cats Protection League charity shop.

It doesn't look like a normal radio, because it isn't a normal radio! It's DAB digital radio so that means it's got a huge display to tell you the name of the DJ or the track you're listening to or just the time if that's all you're after. It's got things that are cooler than a penguin in a snowstorm, like being able to pause the radio to answer your mobile, or even rewind to the start of a track and then record it to SD card. So you can enjoy it over and over until you're sick of it! And then there's all the fabulous stations you can only get on digital radio, like XFM, Smash Hits, 1Xtra, Core, Galaxy, YAAR – you name it! Anyway, enough of me rambling, have a read, and Get The Bug.

Wayne Hemingway

collaboration a product developed by more than one person or business
toils efforts, hard work

New media

Key Reading

> **Persuasion texts**
>
> This is a **persuasion** text. Its **purpose** is to persuade the reader to buy The Bug digital radio.
>
> The main features of this text are:
> - It has a **series of points** supporting a **single viewpoint**, for example, 'And then there's all the fabulous stations you can only get on digital radio…'
> - It has **visual images** to grab the interest of the audience, for example, the cartoon strip.
> - It uses **emotive** and **colourful** language, for example, 'It's got things that are cooler than a penguin in a snowstorm…'
> - It uses **direct address** to gain the attention of the audience and win them over, for example, 'So *you* can enjoy it over and over…'

1 There are two different styles of visual image used in this advert. What are they?

2 'Anyway, enough of me rambling…'

  a) Is this phrase intended to make the reader feel:
  - irritated by Hemingway's rambling
  - comfortable reading his words
  - ready to read on?

  b) How effective is it?

3 The main text could begin, 'The Bug is a really stylish product from Wayne Hemingway and PURE Digital.' What makes the chosen style more effective?

4 Wayne Hemingway addresses the audience directly – 'The Bug is one seriously cool collaboration between yours truly…'

   a) Wayne Hemingway addresses the audience directly in the cartoon as well. Where?

   b) What effect does this direct address have?

Purpose

5 a) What is the main purpose of the cartoon in this persuasion text? Is it:

- to recount a true story of how The Bug was designed
- to attract attention by putting something unusual in an advert
- to entertain the audience by telling a fun story
- to tell you more about the designer of The Bug?

Discuss the answer in small groups and come to an agreement.

   b) Decide whether any of the other purposes also fit this text. Give reasons for your answer.

6 The main text on page 147 tries to persuade the reader to buy The Bug. It does this by making points about how good it is.

   a) Note down four points that the advert makes.

   b) Which do you think is the most persuasive point?

Reading for meaning

The cartoon strip on pages 146 and 147 can be 'read' in many different ways. One reading is simply that it tells a story.

7 Rewrite the story in a single paragraph. You may want to begin like this:

> Wayne Hemingway, the famous designer, was buying a Mars Bar and chips at his favourite chippy one day…

The cartoon can also be 'read' as a way of selling the product. For example:

Suggests he is famous, like a film star

Suggests The Bug is so amazing that people will want to know how it was invented

8 In pairs, 'read' the cartoon on pages 146 and 147 as a way of selling the product. Make notes on each frame, as shown in the example above. Think about what the cartoon is telling you about:
- the product (for example, its quality and style)
- the designer
- the audience (the people who might buy the product).

9 The cartoon also forms part of The Bug website. What differences do you think there are in the web version? (Think about the extra features that technology can add to a text on the Internet.)

> **Exploring further: Close reading**
>
> **10** The cartoon has been designed very carefully. Why do you think the following details have been included:
>
> **a)** the number plate on the kidnappers' van
>
> **b)** the name of the chip shop
>
> **c)** the style of 'THE END….?' in the final frame?

Focus on: Suiting audience and purpose

The Bug advert is written for a particular audience and purpose:

- **audience** – young men and women who like gadgets and style, with money to spare.
- **purpose** – to persuade these people to buy The Bug.

The language of the main text on page 147 is carefully geared to this audience and purpose. For example:

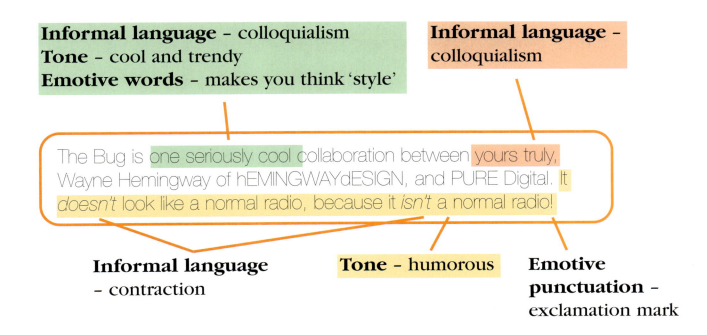

Informal language – colloquialism
Tone – cool and trendy
Emotive words – makes you think 'style'

Informal language – colloquialism

The Bug is one seriously cool collaboration between yours truly, Wayne Hemingway of hEMINGWAYdESIGN, and PURE Digital. It doesn't look like a normal radio, because it isn't a normal radio!

Informal language – contraction

Tone – humorous

Emotive punctuation – exclamation mark

11 In pairs, make notes on the two sentences after '…it *isn't* a normal radio!', to show how the chosen language is suited to its audience and purpose. Remember to look out for the following features:

- **Informal language** – colloquialisms and contractions
- **Emotive language** – words or punctuation to make you feel a certain way
- **Tone** – cool, funny or friendly
- **Direct address** – makes the text personal to *you*.

Exploring further: A different audience

An information text about The Bug would be written in a different way. For example, the language would be more formal, descriptions would not use emotive or colourful words, the tone would be 'straight' and the third person (he/she/it) would mostly be used.

12 Rewrite the first four sentences of the main text of the advert as an information text.
You could begin:
'The Bug is a stylish product from Wayne Hemingway and PURE Digital…'

Key Speaking and Listening

13 You and a partner are top advertising executives. You have been hired by Wayne Hemingway and PURE Digital to come up with a great advertising campaign for The Bug. You dream up the cartoon strip 'The Birth of The Bug'. Now you have to persuade your clients that the cartoon is a great idea. You are going to do this in a spoken commentary.

a) Look back over the work you did on the cartoon strip for questions 8, 9 and 10. Use the notes you made and add any good points from class discussion.

b) Decide how you are going to divide up the presentation. For example, one of you could tell the 'straight' story while the other gives the underlying meaning, one of you could focus on the words and the other on the images.

c) Finally, think about the particular techniques you could use to persuade your audience.
- Use an appropriate tone, direct address and emotive language to win your audience over.
- Try to vary the tone of your voice and the pace of your speech to influence your clients further.

d) Practise your presentation until you are happy with it. Be ready to present the cartoon strip.

2 The Internet – a waste of time?

Aims

- Read a newspaper article that expresses a point of view about the Internet
- Explore how texts like this signpost which way the argument is going (Wr14)
- Think about how and why irony is used in a text (R7)

The following text is an article from *The Independent*.

Don't believe the hype: the Internet's a waste of time

By common consent we are in the middle of a revolution. The Internet revolution differs slightly from the French and Russian revolutions, in that rather than overthrowing the old world order in the quest for liberty and equality for all mankind, this revolution enables you to check the recipes from *Ready, Steady, Cook* without buying the *Radio Times*. What bliss it was to be alive in that dawn.

This week, plans for a new Internet university were announced. This is the latest headline in a long list of wonderful things that a computer and modem can do. There are e-bookshops where you can buy self-help guides to help you deal with the anxiety you felt ever since you divulged your credit card number over the Internet. There are virtual jobs in virtual offices where you go virtually mad never talking to another human being from one day to the next.

Suddenly the Internet is the solution to everything. The Prime Minister is lying awake at night trying to think of a way forward for the troubled peace process in Northern Ireland. "Have you thought about looking on the Internet?" says Cherie. And there it is, instantly available – and all for the price of a local phone call. The way to end world poverty, the secret of eternal happiness, the cure for cancer… apparently you can find out something about almost anything by logging on to the Internet.

The only problem is that when you enter the words "cure" and "cancer", your search engine will find four million sites, the first of which is the diary of a 15-year-old boy from Milwaukee whose favourite band is The Cure and whose star sign is Cancer. And for some reason you find yourself reading ten pages about his trip to summer camp in Vermont before you accept that this site isn't going to have the information you were looking for.

The usefulness of the Internet has been hyped out of all proportion. All it does is make information more easily available. The downside of this is that in doing so it creates an enormous amount of new material, most of which is just information for its own sake. Like mobile phone users on trains on the way to the office, loudly reporting that they are on a train and on their way into the office, much of what is posted on the Internet is up there because it can be, not because it needs to be.

Today libraries are closing while funding for the Internet seems limitless. Is this because we have read all the books there are to read? No, it is simply that the Internet is new. It is so new that even the cynical British have failed to see that it is not a super-highway at all, but the information equivalent of the M25 in the rush hour.

common consent general agreement
divulged revealed
limitless endless
cynical suspicious

Key Reading

Argument texts

This is an **argument** text. Its **purpose** is to express a point of view and persuade the reader to agree with it.

The main features of this text are:

- It makes a **series of points** in a **logical order**, for example, the first paragraph makes the point that computers can do lots of 'wonderful things'.
- It has **topic sentences** that state the main point of each paragraph, for example, in paragraph 1, 'By common consent we are in the middle of a revolution'.
- The main points are backed up by **evidence** or **reasons**, for example, 'And for some reason you find yourself reading ten pages…'
- It uses **formal** but **effective** language, for example, 'Today libraries are closing while funding for the Internet seems *limitless*.'
- It features clear **signposting** of the argument to make the logic clear, for example, 'The only problem is that…'

1 Summarise the author's point of view in one sentence.

2 a) What is the topic sentence in paragraph 2?

  b) What reason does the writer give to back up the main point?

3 What is the main point in the second paragraph? Which sentence makes this clear?

4 The author calls the Internet 'the information equivalent of the M25 in the rush hour' (line 46). What makes this image effective?

5 The phrase 'The only problem is…' (line 28) signposts that the author is about to make an objection to a statement.

   a) What is the statement?

   b) What is the objection?

> **Grammar for reading**
>
> Formal language uses more **complex sentences** than informal language. These are sentences with **more than one clause** that are **linked by connectives**, such as 'so', 'when', 'if' and 'as'.

Purpose

The purpose of an argument text is to put forward a point of view. The author of this article begins by apparently making some points *in favour of* the Internet. For example:

- The Internet has revolutionised our lives (paragraph 1)
- Computers can help people to do lots of wonderful things (paragraph 2).

6 a) What point is being made in favour of the Internet in paragraph 3?

   b) What hints are there that all these points are not actually in favour of the Internet?

7 In the rest of the article, the author makes three points *against* the Internet.

   a) Identify these points and write down a one-sentence summary of each one.

   b) Do all of these points make an effective argument? Give reasons for your answer.

Reading for meaning

Sometimes you think a sentence means one thing and then you realise it means the exact opposite. This is because the **explicit meaning** – the surface or 'obvious' meaning of a text – is not the same as the **implicit meaning** – what the text suggests but doesn't actually say.

For example, look at the following extract from the first half of the newspaper article:

> There are e-bookshops where you can buy self-help guides to help you deal with the anxiety you felt ever since you divulged your credit card number over the Internet.

The **explicit** or **literal meaning** is, 'Here is another example of the many wonderful things available on the Internet.'

The **implicit** meaning is, 'e-bookshops aren't useful at all. The Internet only creates its own problems.'

This is an example of **irony** – when words are used to **imply the opposite** of what they normally mean. It can be a powerful weapon in an argument.

8 In pairs, draw up a chart like the one below. Find at least four more examples of irony in paragraphs 1–3 of the article. Write down the explicit and the implied meaning in each case.

Sentence beginning	Explicit meaning	Implicit meaning
'The Internet revolution differs slightly…'	The Internet is changing our lives, just as other revolutions did.	The things you can do on the Internet are so trivial that it's not at all like the other revolutions.
'This is the latest headline…'	The Internet can do lots of wonderful things.	The things the Internet can do aren't that wonderful.
'There are e-bookshops where you can buy…'	You can even buy books on the Internet.	Buying books on the Internet is no great thing.

9 Discuss why irony is a powerful weapon. Consider these factors:
- humour
- how it affects the opposition's argument.

Exploring further: Rhetorical devices

Some argument texts use more **rhetorical devices** than others. These are techniques used to persuade an audience, for example:
- repetition
- alliteration
- other sound effects.

In the article, the author uses repetition for rhetorical effect.

10 In pairs, discuss the precise effect of the following:

a) The repetition of 'There are…' (paragraph 2)

b) The repetition in the sentence on mobile phone users (paragraph 5)

c) The repetition in 'because it can be, not because it needs to be' (paragraph 5).

Focus on: Signposting arguments

Sentence signposts are phrases at the beginning of a sentence which show the reader where the sentence is going. For example, look at this sentence from paragraph 5 of the article:

Main point

> The usefulness of the Internet has been hyped out of all proportion. **All it does** is make information more easily available.

Sentence signpost: This phrase tells you that the sentence is going to dismiss what the Internet does

Reason given for the main point

11 Look at the next sentence from paragraph 5 of the article. It has a sentence signpost, 'The downside of this is…'. What does this signpost immediately tell you about where the argument is going?

12 Connectives also signpost arguments by making the links between clauses and sentences clear. What job is the connective 'while' doing in the final paragraph of the article?

Key Writing

> Using the Internet allows you to buy things without hitting the High Street.
>
> You can't see the quality of the things you buy over the Internet.

Wr14 **13 a)** Rewrite these statements so that the argument is clear to the reader.
- You could use a simple connective, such as 'but' or 'however'.
- You could use a sentence signpost (see the examples on page 148).
- You may want to keep the two sentences separate or combine them into one sentence.

b) In pairs, come up with four different ways to signpost this argument.

3 Rags to riches

Aims

- Read a true rags-to-riches story
- Remind yourself how recount texts are written
- Investigate how to combine clauses to make your sentences more effective (S1)

The following text comes from *The Scotsman*.

How to make a mobile for-tune

If there is one man who knows just how big ringtones have become then it's Alexander Amosu. The 28-year-old is the man behind the UK's number one provider of phone tunes.

And it's a real rags-to-riches tale. He was born in Britain, but moved to Nigeria at the age of two with his parents. Ten years later, he returned to Britain to live with his grandmother and younger brother.

They moved into a council house in north London and there was so little room, he had to sleep on the sofa in the sitting room. At school, he couldn't relate to the other children who wore Nike and Adidas trainers. He didn't even have enough money for school dinners. "All the kids that everyone liked had the latest gear," he says. "I couldn't fit in. I had really geeky and ugly clothes. I had two options – I could either go in just these trainers or I could work for them."

He got a paper round and bought himself a pair of Nike trainers. His classmates suddenly started talking to him. "From there I thought if I needed something I would just have to work hard for it. I saved the money and kitted myself out to look pretty and before you knew it I was quite popular in school," he says.

While at college he put on parties and set up a house-cleaning business which eventually made more than £1500 a week.

Then, in 2000, when he was just 24, he sent his brother a ringtone he had made on a phone with a composing facility. The tune was Big Pimpin' by Jay-Z, and he had painstakingly keyed in the notes on the phone's keypad.

His brother's phone went off at college and immediately all his friends wanted it. Alexander made them pay £1 for the ringtone. In the first day he made £7. "I thought, this is fantastic! What would happen if I made a catalogue of ringtones and advertised it?" he says. He did some research and found only one company in the UK and several in Germany providing ringtones.

He decided to specialise in R'n'B music and, within six weeks, had come up with a further six ringtones. He installed an extra phone line, with a premium-rate number charging £1.50 a minute, in the council house he was living in with his parents. He advertised the number on the back of 20,000 fliers he made for his next party. On the first day, R'n'B Ringtones made £97. He gave up university.

Within four months he moved the firm into offices in Islington and employed 21 staff, selling 1000 ringtones. "We were making the songs as they were coming out," he says. In the first year turnover was £1.2 million. In 2002, he was named Young Entrepreneur of the Year at the Institute of Directors Black Enterprise Awards.

He now lives in a three-storey townhouse and drives a Porsche. He has also bought homes in Alicante and Nigeria.

facility feature
entrepreneur someone who uses skills and takes risks to set up a business

New media

Key Reading

> **Recount texts**
>
> This text is a **recount** or **chronological report**. Its **purpose** is to recount or tell the reader about a series of events.
>
> The main features of this text are:
> - It is told mainly in the **past tense**, for example, 'He *was* born in Britain…'
> - It describes events in **time order** and refers to **time spans** and **shifts**, for example, '…but moved to Nigeria at the age of two', comes after the information that Alexander was born in Britain.
> - It uses **time connectives**, for example, 'Ten years *later*…'

1 Why is the newspaper interested in Alexander Amosu?

2 a) Where is the first past tense verb in the article?

   b) What tense are the verbs up to this point?

   c) Why have two different tenses been used?

3 a) What did Alexander do in 2000?

   b) What happened to him in 2002?

4 Identify four different time connectives used in this text.

Purpose

5 What do you think is the main purpose of this newspaper article?
- To give you advice on how to make a fortune.
- To show how working hard brings rewards.
- To tell you how Amosu became the number one provider of ringtones.
- To give you information about mobile ringtones.

Point to the evidence in the text that supports your answer.

Reading for meaning

This recount text is written mainly in time order. However, it begins in the present, then 'fast rewinds' to the beginning of Alexander's life. Recounts in newspapers often use **time shifts** like this.

6 Why is the use of time shifts an effective technique in recounts?

7 Look at the newspaper stories below. They also begin in the present tense. Use the 'fast rewind' technique to write the next sentence in each story.

Make sure you have used the past tense.

> **Tornado strikes Norfolk**
> The people of Chatswell are waking up today to a scene of devastation.

> **Murderer released**
> Gerry Giles leaves Wandsworth Prison a free man today.

8 a) Draw up a timeline of events in this recount, like the one below. Start with Amosu's birth and include dates where you can.

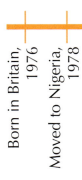

    b) Some events are described in greater detail. Indicate these, using branching lines from the main notes on the timeline.

    c) Why has the writer gone into such detail at these points in the story?

9 a) What do you think the Institute of Directors Black Enterprise Awards are (lines 47–48)?

    b) Why did Alexander Amosu win an award?

'Have' is a very common verb that is used in many different ways. The three main uses of the verb 'have' are:

- It can mean '**possess**' or 'experience'. For example, 'I *have* two sisters' (present tense); 'He *had* a brand-new Ferrari' (past tense).
- It can also mean '**must**' when it is added to another verb. The fact that it works with (adds meaning to) another verb makes it a **modal verb**. For example, 'I *have to go*' (present tense); 'She *had to stop*' (past tense).
- It helps form different **tenses**. For example, 'I *have made* a mistake' (**present perfect** tense); 'I *had made* a mistake' (**past perfect** tense).

10 Identify six uses of the verb 'have' in paragraphs 3–6 of the article. For each use, identify what its job is and what tense it is in.

Exploring further: The present perfect and the past perfect

The **present perfect tense** is made up of the verb '**have/has**' + **the simple past tense**. It shows a link between what happened in the past and what is happening in the present. For example:

The sun *has appeared*.

'Has' + the simple past tense here means that the sun:
- came out in the past
- is still out in the present.

The **past perfect tense** is made up of '**had**' + **the simple past tense**. It refers to something that happened *before* an event in the past. For example:

By 3 o'clock he *had finished* the book.

'Had' + the simple past tense here means that he finished the book *before* 3 o'clock.

Focus on: More effective sentences

In the second paragraph of the article, the author writes:

> He was born in Britain, but moved to Nigeria at the age of two with his parents.

She could have written:

> He was born in Britain. He moved to Nigeria at the age of two with his parents.

However, combining the two sentences has the following advantages:
- It is less repetitive than 'He was born… He moved…'
- The connective 'but' shows how the two clauses are related.
- The new sentence sounds and reads better.

Now look at the next sentence in the second paragraph of the article:

> Ten years later, he returned to Britain to live with his grandmother and younger brother.

11 a) In pairs, discuss why this sentence is better than using two separate sentences.

  b) What connective phrase is used and what does it do?

12 Combine each of the following pairs of sentences.

  a) Ringtones have become big business.
  They have overtaken single CD sales.

  b) People change their ringtones a lot.
  They want to keep up with the charts.

  You will need to:
  - add, cut or change some words
  - link parts of the new sentence with connectives.

  Be prepared to explain what makes your new sentences more effective.

New media

Key Writing

Here are some notes for a short magazine article about Dominic McVey (another young entrepreneur). Your task is to write the article.

> **Dominic McVey**
> Born 1985. At 13, imported motorised scooters from USA. Set up Scooters UK Ltd. Became millionaire at 14. Britain's youngest self-made millionaire.
> **Other business interests:** Manager of boy band *Most Wanted*. Has a web-design business.
> **Ambitions:** Wants to move into politics. Interested in Japanese gaming machines.

- Try to **combine clauses** to make longer sentences.
- **Add connectives** to show how the clauses relate to each other. For example, 'but', 'and', 'however', 'when', 'as', 'since'.
- Use **time connectives** to show any **time shifts** in Dominic's story.
- Add **extra detail** to sentences to give them more interest. For example, you could begin your article:

'Dominic McVey was only a lad of 13 when he began importing motorised scooters from the USA.'

Exploring further

Try adding an extra section to your article on Dominic McVey, to bring his story to life. Include a paragraph on Dominic's first meeting with his clients at an airport in the USA. What is their reaction when they meet the boy they have been trading with?

④ Unit 7 Assignment: The Internet is cool

Assessment Focus

▸ AF3 Organise and present whole texts effectively, sequencing and structuring information, ideas and events

---

> **You:** are writing a letter to the newspaper that printed John O'Farrell's article *Don't believe the hype: the Internet's a waste of time*.
> **Your task:** to put forward the case *for* the Internet.

Stage 1

Brainstorm the reasons why the Internet is cool. You may want to reread the article on pages 154–155. Can you think of your own arguments to undermine those of the author?

You could draw up a spidergram to list your key points, for example:

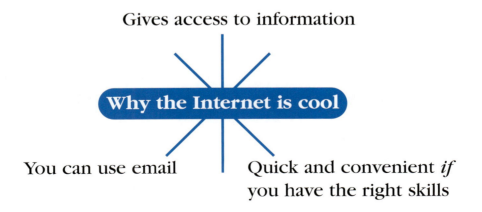

Stage 2

Now plan your letter. Choose your four best points in favour of the Internet. Write down a brief summary of each one.

When drafting your letter, you will write a short paragraph on each of these main points.

- First of all, decide on the best order for your paragraphs.
- Where should your best point go – at the start or the end of your letter?
- Jot down one or two reasons to back up each main point. These may include points against John O'Farrell's arguments or evidence in support of the Internet.
- Construct a text skeleton to plan your argument, like this:

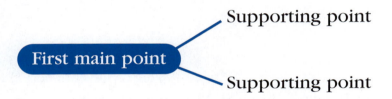

Stage 3

Now draft your paragraphs. Remember to:
- lay them out like a letter to a newspaper
- use formal language
- signpost your argument using connectives or sentence signposts (see page 160), so that the reader knows which way your argument is going.

For example:

Main point, with signposting underlined

Reason given for the main point

One reason the Internet is cool is because you can use email. Email is great because it's so quick.

Now read through your letter again. Can you make any words more powerful or interesting? Can you tighten up your style? For example:

Signpost rephrased to make it snappier

But the coolest thing about the Internet is email. Email beats snail mail hands down.

Reason is rephrased in more colourful language

Challenge

Can you use **irony** to good effect in your letter? How could you use it to:

- undermine the opposing argument
- create humour?

Can you use **rhetorical techniques** in your letter, such as emotive language or repetition?

Robert Clack Comprehensive School
Green Lane, Dagenham, RM8 1AL Essex

Unit 8 Voices from the past

1 "Gas! Gas!"

Aims

- Read an extract from a novel about the First World War
- Develop your understanding of how a writer uses imagery to make effective descriptions (W11)
- Write your own description, using these techniques (Wr5)

This is an extract from *Private Peaceful* by Michael Morpurgo, which is set in the First World War. It is told by a soldier, Thomas Peaceful.

I am writing to Mother – I haven't written for a while and I am feeling guilty about it. My pencil keeps breaking and I am sharpening it again. Everyone else is lying asleep in the sun or is sitting about smoking and chatting. Nipper Martin
5   is cleaning his rifle again. He's always very particular about that.

"Gas! Gas!"

The cry goes up and is echoed all along the trench. For a moment we are frozen with panic. We have trained for
10 this time and time again, but nonetheless we fumble clumsily, feverishly with our gas masks.

"Fix bayonets!" Hanley's yelling while we're still trying frantically to pull on our gas masks. We grab our rifles and fix bayonets. We're on the firestep looking out into
15 no-man's-land, and we see it rolling towards us, this

dreaded killer cloud we have heard so much about but have never seen for ourselves until now. Its deadly tendrils are searching ahead, feeling their way forward in long yellow wisps, scenting me, searching for me. Then finding me out, the gas turns and drifts straight for me. I'm shouting inside my gas mask. "Christ! Christ!" Still the gas comes, wafting over our wire, through our wire, swallowing everything in its path.

I hear again in my head the instructor's voice, see him shouting at me through his mask when we went out on our last exercise. "You're panicking in there, Peaceful. A gas mask is like God, son. It'll work bloody miracles for you, but you've got to believe in it." But I don't believe in it! I don't believe in miracles.

The gas is only feet away now. In a moment it will be on me, around me, in me. I crouch down, hiding my face between my knees, praying it will float over my head, over the top of the trench and seek out someone else. But it does not. It's all around me. I tell myself I will not breathe, I must not breathe. Through a yellow mist I see the trench filling up with it. It drifts into the dugouts, snaking into every nook and cranny, looking for me. It wants to seek us all out, to kill us all, every one of us. Still I do not breathe. I see men running, staggering, falling. I hear Pete shouting for me. Then he's grabbing me and we run. I have to breathe now. I can't run without breathing. Half-blinded by my mask I trip and fall, crashing my head against the trench wall, knocking myself half-senseless. My gas mask has come off. I pull it down, but I have breathed in and know already it's too late.

feverishly in a state of intense excitement
firestep a step that ran along the length of a trench, allowing soldiers to see over the top
no-man's-land the area of land between the two front lines
tendril a thin leaf or stem of a plant that twists around a support

Key Reading

Narrative texts

This is a **narrative** text. Its **purpose** is to tell a story in an entertaining way.

The main features of this text are:

- It has a **structure** that includes an opening (**introduction**), a problem (**complication**), a dramatic moment when everything comes to a head (**crisis**) and an ending (**resolution**) when things are sorted out. For example, the first paragraph (opening) describes the scene before the gas attack.
- It has **characters**, who the story is about. The reader often hears their words and thoughts.
- It has a **narrator**, who tells the story in either the first person (I/we) or the third person (he/she/it). In the extract, the narrator is one of the characters and tells the story in the first person. For example, '*I'm* shouting inside *my* gas mask.'
- It uses **direct speech**. The characters' words are put in speech marks, for example, "You're panicking in there, Peaceful."
- It uses **expressive** and **descriptive language**, for example, 'Its *deadly tendrils* are searching ahead, feeling their way forward in *long yellow wisps*…'

1 What is the narrative about?

2 a) Where does the introduction to this episode end?

　b) There is no gradual development in this episode. Why not?

3 a) How much of this narrative is description and how much is dialogue?

　b) '…we fumble clumsily, feverishly with our gas masks'. What makes this description effective?

4 a) Which words in the first two sentences show that this is a first-person narrative?

b) In a third-person text, the narrator is not a character in the story but writes about other people's experiences. Rewrite the first two sentences as a third-person narrative.

5 The characters' words are quoted directly four times in this passage. Which characters say what?

Purpose

6 What is the main purpose of this text?

a) To write an account of an actual gas attack in the First World War.

b) To tell the reader what gas attacks were like, but in an entertaining way as part of a story.

c) To tell a story of how someone was the victim of a gas attack.

d) To show how terrible war can be.

Point to evidence in the text to support your answer.

Reading for meaning

7 a) What tense are the verbs in this narrative?

b) Why do you think the writer has chosen this tense? What does it bring to the story?

c) Which tense are narratives usually written in?

Exploring further: The present participle

The present participle is the '-ing' form of a verb.
Two of its uses are:

- It forms part of the **continuous present tense**, for example, 'We are *running*…'
- It can **begin a clause** on its own, for example, '*Chatting* away, I did not notice…'

The present participle ('-ing' form) is used four times in this sentence from paragraph 4:

> Its deadly tendrils are *searching* ahead, *feeling* their way forward in long yellow wisps, *scenting* me, *searching* for me.

8 a) Find three more sentences in the extract where the present participle ('-ing' form) is used frequently.

b) What effect do these '-ing' verbs have?

---

9 The focus of the first half of this text is on the group of soldiers as a whole. In the second half of the text, the focus is on Private Peaceful.

a) Scan the text for the first-person pronouns 'we', 'us', 'I' and 'me'. What do you find?

b) Imagine you were directing a film of this book. How could the camerawork reflect this change in focus?

10 Reread the end of the text. What do you think happens to Private Peaceful?

Focus on: Imagery

An image is a picture. **Imagery**, therefore, is the way in which writers help the reader to picture what is going on. They do this by using words and ideas in an imaginative way, and especially by:

- using powerful verbs, nouns, adjectives and adverbs
- comparing things in an unusual way.

Look at this example from paragraph 4 of the extract:

> …we see it rolling towards us, this dreaded killer cloud…

Powerful words

The gas is compared to a cloud. The word implies something dark and threatening

11 In pairs, draw up a table like the one below, to analyse how Michael Morpurgo uses imagery to describe the gas attack in lines 14–22. Make sure you bring out the effect of the **powerful words** and the **comparison** made in each image.

You may want to begin your chart like this:

Description of gas from text (imagery)	Powerful words and effect	Comparison and effect
'…we see it rolling towards us, this dreaded killer cloud…'	rolling – like something mechanical. dreaded – like…	a cloud – something large and threatening

Exploring further: Types of imagery

A **metaphor** is when something is described directly as *being* something else. For example, 'His bedroom *was* a bombsite.'

A **simile** is when something is described as *similar* to something else, using *like* or *as*. For example, 'His bedroom was *like* a bombsite.'

Personification is when an object is described in words that suggest a person or creature. For example, 'He snored, the dog snored, even *his bedroom snored*.'

12 a) Return to the chart you completed for question 11. Highlight the metaphors in your chart. Which do you think is the best one?

b) Find the simile in the instructor's words (lines 25–26).

c) Where is the gas personified in the extract? Why is this idea particularly effective in a war setting?

Key Writing

Tanks were used for the first time in 1916, at the Battle of Flers. They were huge, lumbering machines, but they stunned the German army.

Wr5 **13** You are writing a story from the point of view of a German soldier at the Battle of Flers. You want to describe his first sighting of the tank attack in an effective way.

   a) Discuss with a partner what the picture of the tank on page 178 reminds you of. Use the comparisons you come up with as images in your description.

   - Decide what the tanks are doing as they approach – how do they cope with the terrain? Are they firing at you?
   - Brainstorm some powerful words to include in your description.
   - Use the present tense and first-person pronouns to make the description more vivid.

   b) Working on your own, draft a description of between ten and twelve sentences. You may want to begin like this:

   > We thought it was thunder at first. Hans and I looked at each other, then glanced at the sky. It was cloudless and bright.

   c) Now swap your description with a partner's. Give each other feedback on how effective your descriptions are. Suggest ways in which each other's language and imagery could be improved. Are metaphors, similes or personification used effectively?

   d) Redraft your own description, taking on board your partner's comments.

Voices from the past

2 The silent ship

- Read an extract from a book about the *Mary Celeste* mystery
- Remind yourself of the key features of discursive texts
- Think about the effects of using different tenses (S4)
- Explore different ways of making your writing tentative (S5)

The following text is from a book for young people about the *Mary Celeste*.

The True Mystery of the *Mary Celeste*

Time: Afternoon of 4th December 1872.
Place: The Atlantic Ocean, between the Azores and the coast of Portugal.
Scene: A two-masted sailing ship is spotted by another ship, drifting aimlessly. A small search party boards the ship. They find her to be well-stocked with food and fit to sail, but without a single soul on board.
- The name of this silent ship? The *Mary Celeste*.
- The cause of her passengers' and crew's disappearance? Nobody knows.

Over the years, there have been shiploads of theories to explain the disappearance of the *Mary Celeste's* crew. Here are some of the solutions that have taken the sea-sleuthing world by storm.

Were the missing crewmen kippered by a squid?
In 1904 a magazine article claimed that the entire ship's company had been abducted by a giant octopus! According to the article, the well-armed creature rose from the deep and grabbed the

ship's helmsman. The helmsman's yells brought the rest of the crew up on deck and, one by one, the octopus swept them up.

But could this have been what happened? Well, giant squid can be 20m (60ft) long, with eyes the size of a human head. But if a monster squid is the answer to the riddle, why did all hands remain on deck long enough to be plucked off in turn? And why did the squid make off with the ship's logbook, papers and lifeboat?

Did plundering pirates kill Captain Briggs and his crew?

Some people have suggested that pirates murdered Captain Briggs, his family and crew. But if pirates were to blame, where were the traces of violence you'd expect to see after a raid? And if sea-robbers had swarmed aboard the *Mary Celeste*, why hadn't they looted the ship from stem to stern? Amongst the things found on board were a silver watch, a fancy sword, some gold jewellery and expensive clothes.

Were the crewmen scared witless (and shipless) by an iceberg?

It has been suggested that the crewmen abandoned ship to escape from an iceberg coming their way…although what an enormous chunk of ice was doing floating about the warm waters of the Azores is anyone's guess.

So what is the answer to this unfathomable mystery?

The maddening truth is, we shall probably never be able to prove any likely theory as to the *Mary Celeste's* fate. The clues to its mystery, like its leading characters, are all long gone. Only the sea now knows what really happened on that fateful day in 1872… and the sea keeps its secrets well.

Azores a group of islands
aimlessly with no direction or aim
kippered finished off (in this sense)
abducted snatched, carried off
hands crew
from stem to stern from end to end
unfathomable impossible to solve

Key Reading

Discursive texts

This is a **discursive** text. Its **purpose** is to help someone understand an issue or debate by presenting the arguments fairly.

The main features of this text are:

- It has a form that consists of an **opening statement**, a series of **points** supported by detail or evidence, and a **conclusion**. For example, 'According to the article, the well-armed creature…' introduces a piece of detail.

- It uses **sentence signposts** to signal the view you are writing about, for example, *'Some people* have suggested that…'

- It sometimes uses **tentative language** to suggest different possibilities or ideas, for example, *'But if* pirates were to blame, where were the traces of violence *you'd* expect to see after a raid?'

Grammar for reading

- A **sentence signpost** is a phrase at the beginning of a sentence that helps the reader understand where the sentence is going or its purpose. For example, 'In 1904 a magazine article claimed…'

- **Tentative language** is cautious in its expression. This enables the writer to explore possibilities without stating an idea firmly. For example, phrases such as 'One answer *might* be…' and 'This change *could* mean…'

1 What is the issue or debate in this discursive text? Which section tells you this?

2 a) How many different theories about the crew's disappearance are presented in this text?

b) What conclusion does the writer come to?

3 a) What is the main point made about the first theory in lines 15–19

 b) What extra detail is given to back up this point?

4 What **tentative language** in lines 20–25 suggests that the crewmen may not have been abducted by a giant squid?

5 a) Line 36 begins 'It has been suggested…' What does this sentence signpost tell you about the kind of sentence that is going to follow?

 b) How is the signpost 'Some people have suggested…' in line 27 different from 'It has been suggested…' in line 36?

Purpose

6 What do you think the **main purpose** of this text is?
- To describe exactly what happened to the *Mary Celeste*.
- To present different theories about what happened to the *Mary Celeste* and assess these ideas.
- To dismiss existing theories and come up with a new one.
- To present information about the *Mary Celeste* mystery in an entertaining way.

Point to evidence in the text to support your answer.

Reading for meaning

 7 How does the writer introduce the *Mary Celeste* mystery at the beginning of the text? Discuss:
- the 'fact file' format of the introduction
- the tense of the verbs
- how effective it is as an introduction to a mystery.

The **present tense** is often used in discursive texts to describe what people think now about an issue, for example, 'Here *are* some of the solutions that have taken the sea-sleuthing world by storm' (lines 12–13).

However, most of this text is written in the **past tense**.

8 a) Identify *three* verbs in the past tense.

b) Explain why the author has used this tense.

9 a) How does the author organise her text into sections to make it clear which theory is being discussed?

b) Within each section, where does the author use questions? What effect does this have?

10 What does the author think about the three theories she presents? Point to evidence in the text to support your answer.

The author uses several seafaring terms when alternative terms could have been used. For example, 'there have been *shiploads* of theories…' could be written as 'there have been *loads* of theories…'.

11 a) Write down alternatives for the following terms in the text:
- 'have taken the *sea-sleuthing* world *by storm*' (line 13)
- 'looted the ship *from stem to stern*' (line 31)
- 'this *unfathomable* mystery' (line 40).

b) What is the overall effect of using these terms?

Focus on: The language of possibility

Discursive texts present different theories, views or explanations. The language is often **tentative** since these are *possible theories* rather than facts.

There are several ways in which possibility can be expressed:
- By the **reporting verbs** that introduce the theories. For example, 'a magazine article *claimed* that…'
- By using **modal verbs** such as 'can', 'could', 'may', 'ought' and 'must', which are added to other verbs to suggest possibility or necessity (see also page 182). For example, 'giant squid *can be* 20m (60ft) long…'
- By using **conditional clauses**. These are a clauses beginning with 'if' or 'as long as', which sets the condition for the main clause being true. For example, 'But *if* a monster squid is the answer…'
- By using **words** and **phrases** linked with certainty, such as 'probably'.

12 Reread lines 26–45 of the *Mary Celeste* text.

a) In pairs, note down one example of each type of tentative language listed above (reporting verb, modal verb, conditional clause, words or phrases linked with certainty).

b) Rewrite each example so that it becomes a fact rather than a possibility. Which words do you change or remove in each case?

Exploring further: Introducing facts and theories

When writing a discursive text, you need to make it clear whether you are introducing a fact or a theory. Your choice of sentence signpost is therefore important.

13 Which of the following sentence signposts introduce facts, and which introduce theories?

a) 'His theory is that…'
b) 'It is possible that…'
c) 'According to one view…'
d) 'Research has shown that…'
e) 'It is clear that…'
f) 'It is a fact that…'

Did 'plundering pirates' murder Captain Briggs and the crew?

Key Writing

 14 Here is another theory about what happened to the *Mary Celeste*:

> **Theory:** Captain Briggs went mad and murdered his family and crew before throwing himself into the sea.
>
> **For:** It must have been stressful being cooped up on a small ship. Such an event was reported in 1828.
>
> **Against:** He was a very experienced captain. The ship's lifeboat and logbook were also missing.

Your task is to write a paragraph in the same style as the discursive text, putting forward both sides of this theory.
- Give your paragraph a heading in the form of a question.
- Using a sentence signpost, introduce the theory at the beginning, such as 'Another theory is …'
- Make your language tentative, using modal verbs and conditional clauses.
- Add a sentence or two at the end to make it clear what your opinion is.

Voices from the past

3 Roman Wall Blues

- Read a poem about a Roman soldier
- Remind yourself about the key features of poetry
- Practise using quotations from the poem to back up your points (Wr17)
- Prepare a presentation of the poem to give to the class (S&L3)

The following is a poem by W.H. Auden (1907–1973).

Roman Wall Blues

Over the heather the wet wind blows,
I've lice in my tunic and a cold in my nose.

The rain comes pattering out of the sky,
I'm a Wall soldier, I don't know why.

5   The mist creeps over the hard grey stone,
My girl's in Tungria; I sleep alone.

Aulus goes hanging around her place,
I don't like his manners, I don't like his face.

Piso's a Christian, he worships a fish;
10   There'd be no kissing if he had his wish.

She gave me a ring but I diced it away;
I want my girl and I want my pay.

When I'm a veteran with only one eye
I shall do nothing but look at the sky.

Wall Hadrian's Wall, a Roman wall built across northern England to keep out invaders
Tungria an Italian town
fish used as a symbol by Christians
diced gambled

Key Reading

Poetry

This text is a **poem**. Its **purpose** is to explore feelings and ideas.

A poem is made up of **images**, **rhythm** and **form**.
- The **images** are the pictures made by the words, for example, 'The mist *creeps* over the hard grey stone…'
- The **form** is the framework or pattern of the poem. Poems are written in **lines**, not sentences, for example, the lines of this poem are grouped in twos.
- The **rhythm** is like the beat in music, for example, the line 'I've <u>lice</u> in my <u>tunic</u> and a <u>cold</u> in my <u>nose</u>' has a rhythmic beat. (The underlined words show where the beat falls.)

Other important features of poetry are:
- Some poems **rhyme** and use other **sound effects**, for example, the line endings 'blows'/'nose' and 'sky'/'why' rhyme.
- Some poems are **free verse**. They have lines of different lengths with different rhythms.

1 a) Who is this poem about?

b) Where and when is it set?

2 a) What image or picture do you get when you read the first three lines of the poem?

b) What picture do you get from reading the last two lines?

3. What do you notice about the length of the sentences? How do they fit the pattern of the poem?

Many of the lines are made up of two separate parts. For example, in line 2:

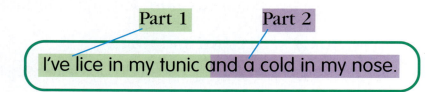

4. What does this add to the poem's overall form?
5. Read the first few lines of the poem out loud.
   a) Where are the main beats (or stresses)?
   b) How many beats are there in each line?
6. There are lots of '-is' sounds in lines 9 and 10. What effect does this sound have? (Think carefully about the soldier's opinion of Piso.)

Purpose

7. a) What do you think is the main purpose of this poem?
   - To give an unusual angle on a famous historical period.
   - To tell a story about a Roman soldier.
   - To give facts about life in Roman Britain.
   - To make you imagine what it was like to be a Roman soldier.
   b) Which of the other purposes also fit this poem? Point to evidence to support your answers.

Reading for meaning

8 a) The poem is written in the first person (i.e. from the point of view of the soldier). What effect does this have?

b) Rewrite a line or two in the third person (he, she, it).

c) Compare the lines written in the first and third person. What do you notice?

9 a) Which lines describe the setting on Hadrian's Wall?

b) What kind of place is it?

c) What do you think the soldier feels about it?

10 Read line 3 of the poem: 'The rain comes pattering out of the sky...' How does the sound of this line help us to picture the scene?

11 The poem quickly moves its focus from the setting to the thoughts of the soldier. Draw a spidergram of all the thoughts and feelings that he has like the example below:

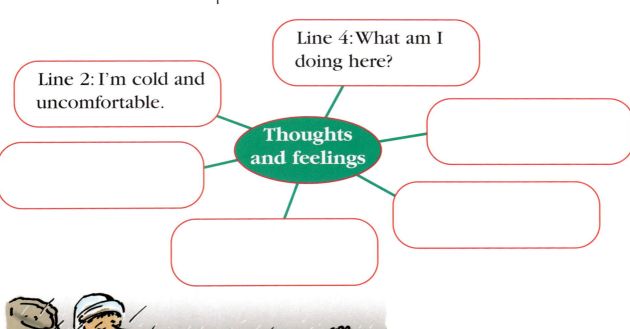

The poem is written in **rhyming couplets**. This is a form of poetry in which lines are written in pairs and has a strong sense of rhythm. Each line in the pair ends with the same sound.

12 a) Explore the effect of the rhyming couplets in the poem.

b) Which of these opinions do you agree with? Or do you have your own views?

> Like most of the words, and the rhythm, the rhyme is simple and straightforward.

> The rhymes are so obvious, almost childish, that it has a comic effect.

> The rhyme is very predictable and plodding, like the rhythm. This is like the boredom of the soldier's life on Hadrian's Wall.

Exploring further: Marking the rhythm

The basic unit of rhythm in this poem is the **dactyl**. In a dactyl, a stressed syllable is followed by two unstressed syllables. For example, in line 9:

```
 /__ _      / _ _    / _ _ /
Piso's a Christian, he worships a fish…
```

Note how three dactyls are followed by a single stressed syllable at the end ('fish').

13 Mark the stresses in line 10: 'There'd be no kissing if he had his wish.' Use the same method as shown in the example above.

Focus on: Using quotations

When you write down or present your ideas about a poem (or any text, for that matter), it is important to support your points with **evidence**. One way in which to do this is to use **quotations** from the text.

When using a quote you should follow these rules:
- Make your point first, then use relevant quotes to support it.
- Only quote short passages – a few words or lines at most.
- Try to work your quote into the sentence, rather than tagging it on as an extra sentence.

For example:

> **Point made clearly at the beginning**
>
> The poem is full of the soldier's worries, which gives it an anxious tone overall. For example, the 'hard grey stone' of the wall makes the soldier think of how hard and grey it is away from his girlfriend. The couplet ends, 'I sleep alone'. 'Alone' sounds as miserable as its rhyme – 'the hard grey stone'.

Evidence is then given for the main point. This includes relevant quotations

- **Quotes** are worked into the sentence, not tagged on as separate sentences
- **Short quotations** are used
- Each quote begins and ends with an **inverted comma**

14 In pairs, you are going to write two or three sentences about the sound effects used in *Roman Wall Blues*.

Wr17

a) First, discuss what sound effects there are.

b) Then work out one or two main points that you want to make.

c) Write down a few quotes to support your point(s). Put a star against the best quotes.

d) Finally, work the quotes into your sentences, as shown in the example above.

Key Speaking and Listening

15 Work in pairs to prepare a presentation of *Roman Wall Blues*. You will need to organise your thoughts about the following aspects of the poem:
- the subject (what it is about)
- the form or structure (how it is laid out)
- the use of rhythm and rhyme
- the message or meaning (why did Auden write the poem?).

a) You should each make short notes on two of these aspects, so that together you cover all four. Try to make two or three main points on each aspect. Jot these down on a prompt card, like the one below.

> **Subject**
> - Roman soldier on sentry duty

b) Make sure you can quote evidence from the text when you make your points. Add relevant quotes to your card.

c) Finally, practise your presentation. Use your card as a prompt – do not read from it directly.

d) Add a sentence or two at the end which gives a personal response to the poem. Say whether you like the poem and remember to give reasons to support your view.

Exploring further

16 Rehearse a reading of *Roman Wall Blues* to bring out the message of the poem and highlight its use of rhythm and rhyme. Then read the poem to the class before giving your presentation.

④ Unit 8 Assignment: The soldier poet

Assessment Focus

◗ AF1 Write imaginative, interesting and thoughtful texts

> **You:** are a poet.
>
> **Your task:** to write a poem about an ordinary soldier in the Second World War.

Stage 1

Your poem will be about the D-Day invasions of France in the Second World War. It will consider this event from your soldier's point of view. Discuss with a partner what you know about the D-Day invasions. The facts below will start you off.

- D-Day was 6 June 1944.
- Its codename was 'Operation Overlord'.
- Two million US, British and Canadian troops made a series of landings on the beaches of Normandy, France.
- Some of the beaches were killing zones – the Germans poured fire onto the troops landing there.

Stage 2

Now you need to get under the skin of your character. What might have been his concerns during (or before) the invasion? Brainstorm his thoughts and feelings with your partner. You could record your ideas in a spidergram like this:

- I feel seasick.
- Will I ever see my girlfriend again?
- **Private X, on the landing craft**
- Will these landing craft work?

Stage 3

Using the ideas you have developed, draft your poem. Follow these tips:

- Your poem should be written in couplets. Aim to write only four or five couplets.
- Give it a strong rhythm and rhyme.
- Focus on the private thoughts and feelings of your character.
- Don't explain in the poem what historical event the soldier is part of. This will be done by your poem's title, so think carefully what you will call your poem.

Challenge

Use **sound effects** in your poem. Apart from using sound effects in rhyme, you could also:

- include **alliteration** (for example, 'shrieking shells')
- use **onomatopoeia** (for example, 'bullets *hissed* past').

Unit 9 Dangerous pursuits

1 Hey dude – what's an extreme sport?

Aims

- Read an information text from a website
- Explore degrees of formality in texts (S12)
- Look at how a text changes when it is made more formal (S10)
- Look at how writers use exaggerated ideas to entertain readers
- Adapt a short information text

The following text comes from a website for young people called *The Site*.

Extreme Sport

TheSite.org

Woooo-yaaaaarggghh! Rad, dude! Like, totally awesome…or something. TheSite.org gets sensible about going wild when it comes to getting fit.

WHAT IS IT?

5   Extreme sports is a loose term to describe any kind of physical activity which has some risk of danger attached to it – from skateboarding to white-water rafting, and freefall parachuting to steep-skiing. It also has to work well with a nu-metal soundtrack.

✌ Chuck in rock-climbing, surfing, wakeboarding, mountain biking and hang gliding, and you begin to realise these are also sports that require guts and reward you with a major adrenalin buzz.

✌ Extreme sports enthusiasts aren't simply on a suicide mission. All such activities demand a high level of skill and control to bring out the best performance. If you wind up in hospital, you're not doing it right.

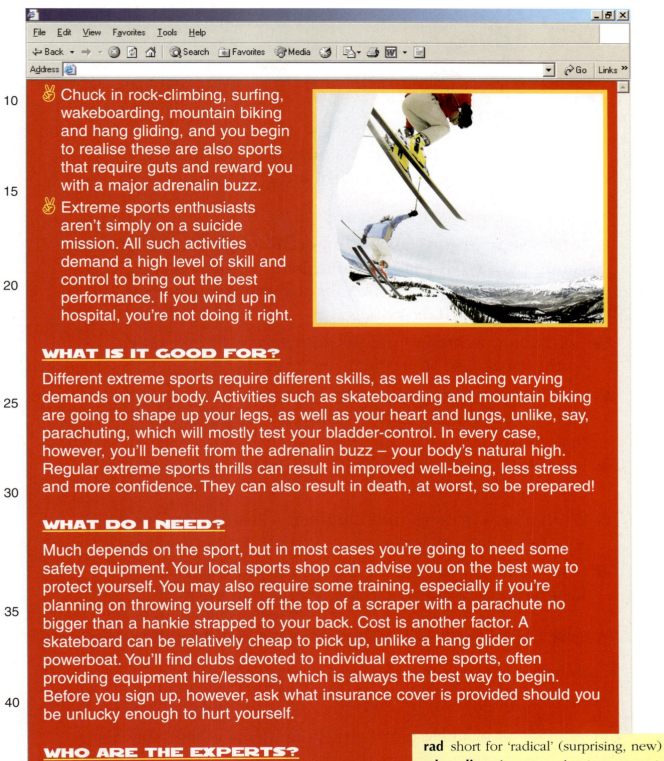

WHAT IS IT GOOD FOR?

Different extreme sports require different skills, as well as placing varying demands on your body. Activities such as skateboarding and mountain biking are going to shape up your legs, as well as your heart and lungs, unlike, say, parachuting, which will mostly test your bladder-control. In every case, however, you'll benefit from the adrenalin buzz – your body's natural high. Regular extreme sports thrills can result in improved well-being, less stress and more confidence. They can also result in death, at worst, so be prepared!

WHAT DO I NEED?

Much depends on the sport, but in most cases you're going to need some safety equipment. Your local sports shop can advise you on the best way to protect yourself. You may also require some training, especially if you're planning on throwing yourself off the top of a scraper with a parachute no bigger than a hankie strapped to your back. Cost is another factor. A skateboard can be relatively cheap to pick up, unlike a hang glider or powerboat. You'll find clubs devoted to individual extreme sports, often providing equipment hire/lessons, which is always the best way to begin. Before you sign up, however, ask what insurance cover is provided should you be unlucky enough to hurt yourself.

WHO ARE THE EXPERTS?

www.thefitmap.com – Links to extreme sports organisations, arranged by category.

www.skateparkpages.co.uk – Find a skate park near you, for skateboarding or BMX.

www.britsurf.co.uk – Surf's up, and this site will sort you out with decent waves, coaching, gear, etc.

rad short for 'radical' (surprising, new)
adrenalin a hormone that is sent out into the body at times of stress or danger
enthusiast someone who loves what they do

Key Reading

Information texts

This is an **information** text. Its **purpose** is to present information on a subject in a clear and/or interesting way.

The main features of this text are:

- It has **clear organisation**. Important or general information is often given first, and the information is arranged in paragraphs or separate sections, for example, 'Extreme sports is a loose term to describe…'
- It is mainly written in the **present tense**, for example, '…these *are* also sports that *require* guts…'
- Other verb tenses may also be used. This text also includes verbs written in the **future tense**, for example, 'you'*ll benefit* from…'
- It often uses **technical terms** or specialist words, for example, 'steep-skiing'.
- It often uses **impersonal language** – that is, language which sounds formal and 'serious', for example, 'Cost is another *factor*.'
- However, it also uses quite **personal** and **informal language**, for example, 'If you *wind up* in hospital…'

1 a) What is the subject of this information text?

  b) Where did the text first appear?

2 Find another example of the present tense under the subheading 'What do I need?'

3 How many specialist extreme sports are mentioned? List them.

4 The very first line of the article uses chatty, informal language. Rewrite this line as a simple, more formal introduction. (You might have to miss out the 'Woooo-yaaaaarggghh' part!) For example, you could start: 'That was fantastic…'

Purpose

The main purpose of this text is to give readers a basic introduction to extreme sports. But what else does it do?

5 Read the table below, which shows three possible additional purposes of the *Extreme Sport* text. Check the text for any evidence of these purposes. Then copy and complete the table, adding the evidence you find.

Purpose	Yes – give evidence	No
To entertain – to make the reader laugh		
To warn of the dangers of some extreme sports		
To encourage the reader to find out more		

Reading for meaning

The text is divided into *four* main sections, each with a different heading.

6 a) Which section deals mainly with equipment and clubs?

b) Which section deals mainly with what extreme sports are?

c) Which section deals mainly with how extreme sports can help people's bodies?

7 How do the headings for these sections help to draw the reader into the text and emphasise what it has to say?

8 What do you think the writer means when she says you will get a 'major adrenalin buzz'?

Dangerous pursuits

Exploring further: Exaggerating to entertain

The problem with information texts is that they can become boring if they're only full of facts and information. The writer of this webpage therefore uses exaggeration, both to make the main points and to make the reader laugh.

9 Read through the text and see if you can identify any exaggerations. Look for:
- a reference to music
- the sort of 'mission' extreme sports enthusiasts aren't really following
- the size of the parachute.

Focus on: Informal and formal texts

Sometimes people write or speak in an **informal** way. For example:

> Oi! Wait up. I'm gonna be there in a mo.

10 How could this be written in a **formal** way (that is, using a less chatty or personal style)? Finish the following version:
'Excuse me. Can you…'

In the information text about extreme sports, the writer wants to make the information *clear*, so some things are written in quite a formal style. However, the text is also written for young people, about young people's sports. So, the writer sometimes writes **informally** and speaks **directly to the reader**.

11 Read Example A and Example B below. One is written in informal language. The other is the same text rewritten in formal language.

a) Which is the informal version?

b) What has been changed in the formal version? Try to be as precise as possible.

Example A

> Chuck in rock-climbing, surfing, wakeboarding, mountain biking and hang gliding, and you begin to realise these are also sports that require guts…

Example B

> Include rock-climbing, surfing, wakeboarding, mountain biking and hang gliding, and one realises that these are also sports that require bravery…

12 Listed below are other informal words or phrases from the text on pages 198–199. Write down some formal alternatives for each word or phrase:

- 'totally awesome'
- 'a major buzz'
- 'if you wind up in hospital'
- 'hankie'.

Key Writing

S12 **13** Your task is to help make the following text (which is written for young climbers) more suitable for older people.

a) Read through the text. The informal sections have been highlighted.

> Climbing is a well-cool thing to do. When I'm perched on top of some peak, I feel like a million dollars, but you don't get there by luck.
>
> You gotta get real. If you wanna get a buzz out of it, you need to do it safely.
>
> You'll need the proper stuff – and the right guys around you. It's no use being surrounded by your mates who have never seen a mountain in their lives.
>
> Nah. I reckon you need expert help. Dudes who know what they're blabbin' on about.

b) Now rewrite the text so that it is suitable for adults and older people. You may have to change more than just the selected words – it might be easier and more effective to rewrite the whole sentence, or to add more information. For example, 'You gotta get real' might need to become 'It is important to be realistic about what is required.'

Exploring further

More formal and impersonal texts tend not to mention 'you' or 'I' so much. However, changing these references can prove tricky.

For example, look at the short extract opposite from an information text on climbing. Note how the first phrase has been changed to a more impersonal style.

Replace '*When I'm*' with '*Being*'

> ~~When I'm~~ perched on top of some peak, I feel like a million dollars, but you don't get there by luck.

14 Change or remove the remaining personal references, such as 'I' and 'you', from the extract. Replace them with more formal and impersonal words such as 'it' and 'this', or take out/change other words.

How to do a bungee-jump

Aims

- Read an explanation text that also uses instructions
- Revise and develop your skills as a critical reader (R4)
- Perform a commentary (S&L4)

The following text comes from a science website. It is about bungee-jumping – the sport where people leap from bridges, buildings or aircraft, attached to a long elastic lead.

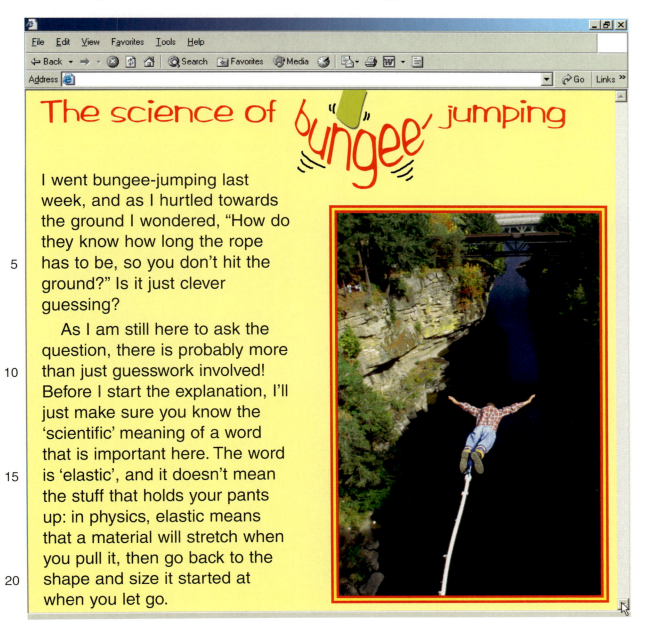

The science of bungee-jumping

I went bungee-jumping last week, and as I hurtled towards the ground I wondered, "How do they know how long the rope has to be, so you don't hit the ground?" Is it just clever guessing?

As I am still here to ask the question, there is probably more than just guesswork involved! Before I start the explanation, I'll just make sure you know the 'scientific' meaning of a word that is important here. The word is 'elastic', and it doesn't mean the stuff that holds your pants up: in physics, elastic means that a material will stretch when you pull it, then go back to the shape and size it started at when you let go.

205

Now, let's do a bungee-jump in miniature. Get a long, thin elastic rubber band, and hang it from a hook or a door handle; that's the bungee rope. Next, put a weight on the bottom end of the band – a lump of plasticine will do; that's you. (I know you don't look like a lump of plasticine, but this is just an experiment, so either use your imagination or your artistic talent to sort it out.) What's happened? Correct! The rubber band has stretched. It is now longer than when we started, because the force (weight) of the plasticine is pulling down on the end. However, that's you at the end of the jump. What about the 'Jump off the bridge and shout "Neeeyaaargh!"' part at the start?

If you lift the plasticine and then drop it, you will see it goes lower because the band stretches more, then it gets shorter and jerks the plasticine up again. The elastic rope does the same to you, and you bounce up and down a few times before you stop.

If you do the same thing again, the plasticine will go down the same distance each time before it is pulled up. This happens because the rubber band stretches more for a big force than it does for a small force, but it always stretches the same amount with the same force.

When you jump off a bridge on a bungee-rope, the experts have worked out, with some clever maths, exactly how much your weight will stretch the rope as you fall. (This is something you can do with elastic materials, using a discovery made by Robert Hooke.) They can measure just the right length to make sure that you get very close to the river, ground or whatever is under the bridge, but you don't actually hit it. Of course, bungee-jumpers should never lie about their weight!

Key Reading

Explanation texts

This text is mainly an **explanation** text. Its **purpose** is to explain how something happens in a clear way. However, in order to do this it also includes **instructions**.

The main features of this text are:

- It has a series of **clear and logical steps**, for example, the first and second paragraphs of the website make it clear exactly what this text is setting out to explain.

- It uses **causal language**, which shows how one thing causes another. For example, in the sentence 'you will see *it goes lower* because the band stretches more…', the phrase 'because the band stretches more' describes the **cause** and the phrase 'it goes lower' describes the **effect**.

- It uses **formal** and **impersonal language** that often includes **technical** and **specialist** words and phrases, for example, 'It is now longer than when we started, because the *force* (weight) of the plasticine is pulling down on the end.'

- It is written mainly in the **present tense** when making general points or explaining rules, for example, '…it always *stretches* the same amount with the same force.'

- Other verb tenses may also be used. This text also includes verbs written in the **past tense** and the **present perfect tense**, to explain an effect, for example, 'What's *happened*? Correct! The rubber band *has stretched*…'

Dangerous pursuits

1. The writer uses an experiment to explain how a bungee-jump works.
   a) What are the main materials in the experiment?
   b) What do they replace from the 'real' jump?

2. Find a sentence in paragraph 5 that describes why something happens (the cause).

3. Find an example of the present tense in paragraph 3.

4. The explanation does not contain many technical terms. However, the writer does explain the scientific meaning of the word 'elastic'. Explain what this word means to a partner.

Purpose

The main purpose of this text is to explain *how* and *why* something happens. However, there are also moments when the writer *instructs* the reader.

5. What does the writer give instructions about?

We can tell that the writer is giving instructions from the sorts of words and phrases he uses. For example, he uses **imperative verbs**. He also uses **time** and **sequence connectives**.

6 Find as many examples of imperative verbs and time and sequence connectives as you can from paragraphs 2 and 3 of the website.

> **Grammar for reading**
>
> **Imperative** verbs tell (or **command**) you directly to do something, for example, '*Take* a long piece of tubing'. **Time** and **sequence connectives** show the order in which things must be done, for example, '*Next* take a long piece of tubing …'.

7 The text on pages 205–206 comes from a science website that is really showing what 'elastic' and 'force' mean. How does the writer stop his explanation from becoming boring?

In pairs, find examples of the writer doing each of the following:
- telling readers about something he did in his own life
- mentioning another type of elastic that readers might find funny
- asking readers direct questions, as though he is talking to them.

Reading for meaning

8 At the end of the text the writer mentions some 'clever maths' done by some experts, and a 'discovery' by Robert Hooke. Why doesn't he explain this maths and this discovery in any detail? Think carefully about the audience (the readers) and the purpose of the text.

9 Because this is a text about force and its effect, it contains lots of movement words. For example, in paragraph 1 the writer describes how he 'hurtled' towards the ground on his bungee-jump. Why is 'hurtled' a more effective verb than 'fell'?

10 Many explanation texts also include a range of design features, such as bullet-points or diagrams. In pairs, list any other design features you might see in explanation texts.

Exploring further: Improving the layout

11 Working on your own, reread the website text. Note down as many ways as you can of improving the layout.
- Refer to the list of design features you created for question 10.
- Sketch out your ideas on a sheet of A4 paper. You needn't copy out the whole text: simply use block shading (or the first words of the paragraph) to show where the text goes.

Focus on: Writing your own explanation or commentary

As you have seen, good explanation texts are able to **make processes clear**. Part of the way this is done is by **showing cause and effect**.

Read this voice-over for a science television programme:

During such programmes, experts often speak using the **present tense** to describe and explain what they see. For example:

Here we are, driving through the African bush, *looking* for a pride of lions.

12 Read the following short sentences:
- We camped near the caves. We could see the bats at night-time.
- I stood near the edge of the cliff face. I could just see the chicks emerging from the nest.
- We travelled a long distance. We needed to be on the river early the next morning.

a) Link these short sentences together to bring out the cause and effect. Choose from the following connectives:
- as
- so
- that
- in order to
- as a result.

b) Then change the verb used from the past to the present tense. For example, 'camped' becomes 'are camping'.

Key Speaking and Listening

S&L4 **13** The four images below show somebody doing a skateboard trick – the 'Acid Drop' or 'Drop Off'. Explain to a friend *how* to do it, using the captions to help you.

1 The right place. *This is perfect.*
2 Both feet on board.
3 Using the tail.
4 Moving feet into position.

For example:

> **Picture 1:** Here I am doing the Acid Drop. It's best to find a drop followed by a flat surface when you start, because if it's too steep it's difficult to control your board.
>
> **Picture 2:** Now, here I am...

Remember to:
- use the present tense
- use connectives to show cause and effect
- include any technical terms that are required
- use some informal language to make it interesting for your audience.

Exploring further

14 Imagine that you are giving the talk above to some seven- to eight-year-olds. Discuss in pairs which of the following formats would be best for the commentary, and why:
- A live demonstration, with a friend doing the moves while you explain
- A PowerPoint presentation
- A video with a voice-over
- A display of photos on a projector screen.

Dangerous pursuits

Touching the void

Aims

- Read an exciting real-life account to do with climbing
- Explore different types of sentences and their effects on the reader (S2)
- Write your own recount text

The following text is from a book by Joe Simpson about two men on a climbing trip that goes terribly wrong. In this section, Simon is wondering what has happened to his companion, Joe, who has fallen down the ice. He can't see him but he can feel him hanging from the end of the rope below.

As the rope ran out I realised that the pressure wasn't easing. Joe was still hanging free. What in hell's name was I lowering him over?

I looked down at the slack rope being fed through the belay plate. Twenty feet below I spotted the knot coming steadily towards me. I began swearing, trying to urge Joe to touch down on to something solid. At ten feet I stopped lowering. The pressure on the rope hadn't changed.

I kept stamping my feet. I was trying to halt the collapse of the seat but it wasn't working. I felt the first shivers of fear. Snow hit me again from behind, surging over and around me. My thighs moved down fractionally. The avalanche pushed me forward and filled the seat behind my back. Oh God! I'm coming off!

Then it stopped as abruptly as it had started. I let the rope slide five feet, thinking furiously. Could I hold the rope with one hand below the knot and change the plate over? I lifted one hand from the rope and stared at it. I couldn't squeeze it into a fist. I thought of holding the rope locked against the plate by winding it round my thigh and then releasing the plate from my harness. Stupid idea! I couldn't hold Joe's weight with my hands alone. If I released the plate, 150 feet of free rope would run unstoppably through my hands, and then it would rip me clear off the mountain.

It had been nearly an hour since Joe had gone over the drop. I was shaking with cold. My grip on the rope kept easing despite my efforts. The rope slowly edged down and the knot pressed against my right fist. I can't hold it, can't stop it. The thought overwhelmed me. The snow slides and wind and cold were forgotten. I was being pulled off. The seat moved beneath me, and snow slipped away past my feet. I slipped a few inches. Stamping my feet deep into the slope halted the movement. God! I had to do something!

The knife! The thought came out of nowhere. Of course, the knife. Be quick, come on, get it.

The knife was in my sack. It took an age to let go a hand and slip the strap off my shoulder, and then repeat it with the other hand. I braced the rope across my thigh and held on to the plate with my right hand as hard as I could. Fumbling at the catches on the rucksack, I could feel the snow slowly giving way beneath me. Panic threatened to swamp me. I felt in the sack, searching desperately for the knife. My hand closed round something smooth and I pulled it out. The red plastic handle slipped in my mitt and I nearly dropped it. I put it in my lap before tugging my mitt off with my teeth. I had already made the decision. There was no other option left to me. The metal blade stuck to my lips when I opened it with my teeth.

I reached down to the rope and then stopped. The slack rope! Clear the loose rope twisted round my foot! If it tangled it would rip me down with it. I carefully cleared it to one side, and checked that it all lay in the seat away from the belay plate. I reached down again, and this time I touched the blade to the rope.

It needed no pressure. The taut rope exploded at the touch of the blade, and I flew backwards into the seat as the pulling strain vanished. I was shaking.

Leaning back against the snow, I listened to a furious hammering in my temple as I tried to calm my breathing. Snow hissed over me in a torrent. I ignored it as it poured over my face and chest, spurting into the open zip at my neck, and on down below. It kept coming. Washing across me and down after the cut rope, and after Joe.

I was alive, and for the moment that was all I could think about. Where Joe was, or whether he was alive, didn't concern me in the long silence after the cutting. His weight had gone from me. There was only the wind and the avalanches left to me.

When at last I sat up, the slack rope fell from my hips. One frayed end protruded from the belay plate – he had gone. Had I killed him? I didn't answer the thought, though some urging in the back of my mind told me that I had. I felt numb. Freezing cold, and shocked into a numb silence, I stared bleakly into the swirling snow beneath me wondering at what had happened. There was no guilt, not even sorrow. I stared at the faint torch beam cutting through the snow and felt haunted by its emptiness.

---

belay plate mountaineering equipment used to secure a rope

avalanche mass of snow and ice descending a mountainside

harness straps for attaching equipment to the body

mitt a thick, protective glove

Dangerous pursuits

Key Reading

Recount texts

This text is a **recount**. Its **purpose** is to tell the reader about a series of real events, so that they can understand what happened.

The main features of this text are:

- It is written in the **past tense**, for example, 'I *looked* down at the slack rope…'
- Events are presented in **time (chronological) order**, for example, 'It *had been nearly an hour* since Joe had gone over the drop.'
- It uses **time connectives**, for example, 'When *at last* I sat up, the slack rope fell from my hips.'
- The **paragraphs** generally show a **change in focus**, for example, the fifth paragraph ends 'I had to do something!' and the next paragraph begins 'The knife! The thought came out of nowhere.'
- It uses **powerful descriptive language**. There are many examples in this text:
  '…shocked into a *numb* silence…' (adjective)
  'My thighs moved down *fractionally*' (adverb)
  'The thought *overwhelmed* me' (verb).

1 The text concerns two men. Which one is recounting what happened?

2 This text isn't just about what happened. It is also about the writer's feelings and emotions. Find an example that tells us how the writer feels in paragraph 7.

3 In paragraph 4, one time connective is used twice to help the reader understand *when* things are happening. What is it?

4 Find two examples of an adverb in paragraph 4.

Purpose

The writer clearly wants to tell the reader what happened. To gain the reader's interest and keep it, he describes:

- the **drama and tension** of what happened
- the **emotions** going through his mind
- the **exact events** in detail, so that the **key moment** in the text makes sense.

5 What do you think is the writer's main purpose in this extract?

    a) To describe what it's like on an icy mountain.
    b) To explain what led to the cutting of the rope.
    c) To tell the reader how difficult mountaineering is.
    d) To describe conditions during an avalanche.

Point to the evidence in the text that supports your answer.

Reading for meaning

The text is full of descriptions of the conditions on the mountain and of the writer's state of mind.

6 Look at the information in the table on page 218. Column 1 contains descriptions of the writer's different states of mind (feelings or emotions). Your task is to copy and complete the second column of the table by finding evidence from the text to match each of these states.

- One piece of evidence of each feeling or emotion will do, but you can add more if you wish.
- A piece of evidence has already been entered in the table, as an example.

Dangerous pursuits

Writer's state of mind (feelings or emotions)	Evidence from the text
Feeling foolish	
Not concerned	'Snow hissed over me in a torrent. I ignored it as it poured over my face and chest...'
Desperate, in a panic	
Relieved	
Other feelings or emotions	

Focus on: Different sentence structures

The writer uses many different types of sentence to get across what happens and how he feels. Here is one example:

> The knife! The thought came out of nowhere. Of course, the knife. Be quick, come on, get it.

This series of short sentences shows how the thought about the knife *suddenly* appears in the writer's mind. The paragraph could have been written like this:

> Suddenly, I had a good idea which was that I could use the knife, so I decided to get it.

S2 **7** Why is the first version *better* than the second version?

Sometimes a longer sentence is more suitable to explain in detail what happened. For example, 'I felt in the sack, searching desperately for the knife.'

This sentence is made up of two **clauses**:

- The **main clause** describes the main action. This clause is complete and could be a sentence on its own.
- The second clause is a **non-finite clause**. It comes after the comma and could not be a sentence on its own. The use of the continuous present verb 'searching' is very important because it describes what the writer is doing *while* he feels in the sack.

Main clause: I felt in the sack,
Continuous present verb 'searching'
Non-finite clause: *searching* desperately for the knife.

Usually, these sorts of sentences can be swapped around. For example:

Searching desperately for the knife, I felt in the sack.

S1

8 a) Identify the non-finite clauses in these two sentences:

- Fumbling at the catches on the rucksack, I could feel the snow slowly giving way beneath me.
- Leaning back against the snow, I listened to a furious hammering in my temple as I tried to calm my breathing. (Think about where the comma is.)

b) For each sentence, identify the continuous present verb.

Dangerous pursuits

Key Writing

9 Imagine you are Joe, at the bottom of the rope. Suddenly you realise it has been cut!
Describe what happens next. Finish each of the sentences below by adding a clause – either a **main clause** (which could make a sentence on its own) or a **non-finite clause**.

a) 'Hanging onto the rope, I suddenly…' (Add a simple verb and more detail.)

b) 'I plunged through the air…' (Add a continuous verb ending in '-ing' and more detail.)

c) 'Reaching out for something to hold, I could feel…' (Add more detail to complete the sentence.)

10 Now continue the story of what happened to Joe (up to 175 words). You can include the sentences above but should add more detail. You could start with:

> I had been stuck swinging on the end of the rope ever since the fall. Every now and again the rope slipped but I was still hundreds of feet above the ground. Hanging onto the rope, I suddenly…

220

④ Unit 9 Assignment: Explorer

Assessment Focus

⟩ AF3 Organise and present whole texts effectively, sequencing and structuring information, ideas and events

You: are an explorer, back from a dangerous expedition. You have been tracing Captain Scott's return journey from the South Pole with one other person, Sam Brooker.

Your task: to write an account of a particularly dangerous moment from your journey. It will form part of a chapter from a book you are writing.

Stage 1

Look at the notes you made during the expedition.

Notes

Day 24 – Blizzard.
On the Beardmore Glacier.
Heading for the Ross Sea.
Temperature –28°F (–2°C).
Sam has fever, can't go on.
I search for painkillers in rucksack – only have five tablets left; almost lose them.
We pitch camp, and I call for assistance.
Weather so bad helicopter cannot find us or land.
We decide to try to get out of glacier before temperature drops any more.
I pull Sam on a sled behind me.
He's looking bad.
Stop and check satellite navigation system.
Isn't working. Can't go on.
Suddenly helicopter appears out of nowhere and lands. Saved!

Stage 2

Plan your first paragraph: decide what it's going to be about. For example, 'Date and location. Me walking through the snow; Sam behind me then falling to the ground…'

Then plan more paragraphs in the same way. If it helps, use a timeline like the one on the next page to organise your notes. Then decide where the paragraph breaks will come and mark them as zig-zags across the time line.

Me walking in snow, Sam falling to ground

Stage 3

Now draft each of your paragraphs. Remember to:

- Use the past tense (*not* the present tense, which the notes are written in).
- Start with a verb ending '-ing', for example, '*Staggering* through the snow, I turned…'
- Add at least one short sentence, for example, 'Then I saw him. Sam! On the frozen ground!'
- Include time connectives, such as 'then', 'next' and 'afterwards', to make it clear to the reader what happens when.
- Add some powerful description to give detail and build up tension, for example, 'Then I saw him. Sam! On the frozen ground – helpless and unable to raise his exhausted body.'

Challenge

Turn your work into a longer piece of writing. To do this, you should recount more of your expedition, perhaps adding:

- why you were there
- what happened *earlier* in the journey
- what happened *after* the helicopter rescued you.

To gain more facts for your writing, you may need to research information on Antarctica and Captain Scott's last expedition, using books or a range of information sources.

William Collins' dream of knowledge for all began with the publication of his first book in 1819. A self-educated mill worker, he not only enriched millions of lives, but also founded a flourishing publishing house. Today, staying true to this spirit, Collin packed with inspiration, innovation and practical expertise. They place you at the centre of a world of possibility and give you exactly what you need to explore it.

Collins. Do more.

Published by Collins
An imprint of HarperCollins*Publishers*
77–85 Fulham Palace Road
Hammersmith
London
W6 8JB

Browse the complete Collins catalogue at
www.collinseducation.com

© HarperCollins*Publishers* Limited 2004

10 9 8 7 6 5 4 3 2 1

ISBN 0 00 719436 6

Mike Gould, Mary Green, John Mannion and Kim Richardson assert their moral rights to be identified as the authors of this work

All rights reserved. No part of this publication may be reproduced, stored in a retrieval system, or transmitted in any form or by any means, electronic, mechanical, photocopying, recording or otherwise, without the prior written permission of the Publisher or a licence permitting restricted copying in the United Kingdom issued by the Copyright Licensing Agency Ltd., 90 Tottenham Court Road, London W1T 4LP.

British Library Cataloguing in Publication Data
A Catalogue record for this publication is available from the British Library

Acknowledgements

The following permissions to reproduce material are gratefully acknowledged:

Text: Extract from 'Dracula' by Bram Stoker, pp4-5; 'Alternative Endings to an Unwritten Ballad' by Paul Dehn, © The Estate of Max Beerbohm, reprinted by permission of Berlin Associates, pp12-13; extract from 'The Pig Scrolls' by Paul Shipton, (Puffin Books 2004) © Paul Shipton 2004, pp28-29; extract from '10 urban myths to chill you to the bone' from ivillage.co.uk, p35; extract from 'How Urban Legends Work' by Tom Harris from howstuffworks.com, pp35-36; extract from 'Robin Hood: Prince of thieves or just a petty thief?', from The National Museum of Australia website at nma.gov.org, pp42-43; extract from 'The Hook' by Kevin Crossley-Holland, OUP 1998, p49; extract from 'The Lord of the Rings' by J. R. R. Tolkien, reprinted by permission of HarperCollins Publishers Ltd © Tolkien 1954, pp52-53; 'The Nose' by Iain Crichton-Smith , from 'In the Middle' (Victor Gollancz Ltd 1977), pp59-60; Derren Brown's Tricks of the Mind, an Objective Productions production for Channel 4. Extract from Channel4.com courtesy of Channel 4 Television, pp66-67; extract from 'Hurricanes and Tornadoes' by Neil Morris (Ticktock Media 1999), pp74-75; extract from 'Tea Pests' by J. W. Beagle Atkins (William Blackwood and Sons Ltd), pp81-82; extract from 'The Birds' by Daphne du Maurier, taken from 'The Birds and Other Stories' (Penguin,1968), pp88-89; extract from 'Billy Elliot' by Lee Hall (Faber and Faber 2000), pp98-99; 'Writing for the Simpsons', from tinyonline.co.uk, pp105-106; extract from 'My Family brings humour to Christmas Day' from tvtoday.co.uk, pp112-113; extract from 'Refugee Boy' by Benjamin Zephaniah (Bloomsbury 2001), with permission from Bloomsbury Publishing, pp122-123; 'Refugees and Asylum Seekers – the Facts' from the Council for Racial Equality website at cre.gov.uk, pp129-130; STAR campaign leaflet reproduced with permission, pp135-136; extract from 'The Birth of The Bug' reproduced with permission of Pure Digital, pp146-147; extract from 'Don't believe the hype' by John O'Farrell, The Independent Newspaper, 17th February 2000, pp154-155; extract from 'So annoying, but they bring in the money' by Gina Davidson, reproduced with permission from The Scotsman Publications Limited, pp162-163; extract from 'Private Peaceful' by Michael Morpurgo, reprinted by permission of HarperCollins Publishers Ltd © Michael Morpurgo 2003, reproduced with permission from HarperCollins Publishers pp172-173; extract from 'The True History of the Mary Celeste' by Rachel Wright (Scholastic, 2001), reproduced with permission from Scholastic Ltd, pp180-181; 'Roman Wall Blues' from 'Collected Poems' by W. H. Auden (Faber and Faber) reproduced with permission from Faber and Faber, p188; 'Extreme Sport', reproduced with permission from thesite.org, pp198-199; 'The science of bungee jumping', from sciencenet.org.uk, pp205-206; extract from TOUCHING THE VOID by Joe Simpson published by Jonathon Cape. Used by permission of the Random House Group Limited, pp214-221.

Images: Alamy Ltd: Aquarius: pp22, 55, 57, 98, 101, 103, 105, 109, 111, 119; Alasdair Bright, NB Illustration: pp7, 8, 15, 16, 51, 191, 192, 212; Andy Ward, NB Illustration: pp59, 64; Aquarius Collection: pp; BBC: pp112, 116, 117; Corbis: pp124, 128, 199, 203, 205, 206, 208, 211, ; Getty Images: pp25, 35, 74, 77, 79, 87, 88, 90, 92, 97, 129, 139, 140, 142, 143, 154, 158, 161, 167, 171, 221; Kobal Collection: pp214, 220, Marco Schaaf, NB Illustration: p72; Mary Evans Picture Library: pp19, 43, 46, 175, 183, 185, 186; Matt Carr: pp65, 68; Movie Store Collection Ltd: pp24, 28, 45; PA Photos: p132; Popperfoto: pp178, 196; Sarah Naylor, NB Illustration: pp31, 34.

Whilst every effort has been made both to contact the copyright holders and to give exact credit lines, this has not proved possible in every case.

Printed and bound by Printing Express, Hong Kong